The Street-wise Popular Practical Guides

EER Street-wise Guides, No. 7.

The Street-wise Guide to The Devil and His Works

Stephen Davies

EER
Edward Everett Root, Publishers, Brighton, 2021.

EER

Edward Everett Root, Publishers, Co. Ltd.,
Atlas Chambers, 33 West Street, Brighton, East Sussex, BN1 2RE.
Details of our overseas agents, and also how to order our books, are given on our website. www.eerpublishing.com

edwardeverettroot@yahoo.co.uk

EER Street-wise Guides, no.7.

Stephen Davies

The Street-wise Guide to The Devil and His Works

First published in Great Britain in 2021.

© Stephen Davies, 2021.

This edition © Edward Everett Root Publishers 2021.

ISBN: 978-1-911454-76-2 Paperback.
ISBN: 978-1-911454-77-9 Hardback.
ISBN: 978-1-911454-80-9 eBook.

Stephen Davies has asserted his right to be identified as the author of this Work in accordance with the Copyright, Designs and Patents Act 1988 as the owner of this Work.

All rights reserved. No part of this publication may be reproduced, stored in a retrieval system or transmitted in any form or by any means, electronic, mechanical, photocopying, recording or otherwise, without the prior permission of the copyright owner.

Typeset in Book Antiqua

Book production by Pageset Limited, High Wycombe, Bucks.

The Street-wise Popular Practical Guides
Edited by Karol Sikora and John Spiers.

This original paperback series provides *practical,* expert, insider-knowledge.

Each book tells you what professionals know, but which is not often shared with the public at large.

The books provide vital insider guidance, including what some authorities would prefer you never to know.

The series empowers the individual.

The authors are all internationally acknowledged professional experts and skilled popular writers.

We will be pleased to receive suggestions for other titles.

AVAILABLE.

Eamonn Butler, *The Street-wise Guide to the British Economy.*

Georgina Burnett, *The Street-wise Guide to Buying, Improving, and Selling Your Home.*

Stephen Davies, *The Street-wise Guide to the Devil and His Works.*

Robert Lefever, *The Street-wise Guide to Coping with and Recovering from Addiction.*

Karol Sikora, *The Street-wise Patient's Guide To Surviving Cancer. How to be an active, organised, informed, and welcomed patient.*

Gill Steel, *The Street-wise Guide to Getting The Best From Your Lawyer.*

Lady Teviot, *The Street-wise Guide to Doing Your Family History.*

FORTHCOMING.

Raj Persaud and Peter Bruggen, *The Street-wise Guide to Getting the Best Mental Health Care. How to Survive the Mental Health System and Get Some Proper Help.*

Nung Rudarakanchana, *The Street-wise Woman's Guide to Getting The Best Healthcare.*

The Author

Dr. Steve Davies is the Head of Education at the Institute of Economic Affairs (IEA) in London. Previously he was program officer at the Institute for Humane Studies (IHS) at George Mason University in Virginia. He joined IHS from the UK where he was Senior Lecturer in the Department of History and Economic History at Manchester Metropolitan University. He has also been a Visiting Scholar at the Social Philosophy and Policy Center at Bowling Green State University, Ohio.

An historian, he graduated from St Andrews University in Scotland in 1976 and gained his PhD from the same institution in 1984. He has authored several books, including *Empiricism and History* (Palgrave Macmillan, 2003) and was co-editor with Nigel Ashford of *The Dictionary of Conservative and Libertarian Thought* (Routledge, 1991).

His most recent and acclaimed work is *The Wealth Explosion. The Nature and Origins of Modernity*, published by EER.

Contents

Introduction 1

Chapter 1. The Devil: The Basic Idea 5

Chapter 2. The Origins of the Devil 17

Chapter 3. The Devil in the Middle Ages 31

Chapter 4. The Renaissance and the Transformation of
            The Devil 45

Chapter 5. The Devil in the Modern World 57

Chapter 6. The Devil's Residence: Hell 75

Chapter 7. The Devil's Allies: Demons, Demonology,
            and Creatures of the Dark 91

Chapter 8. The Devil's Servants: Witches, Warlocks,
            and Witch Hunts 109

Chapter 9. Contemporary Satanism – Followers and
            Admirers of the Devil Today 127

Chapter 10. The Devil in Art and Literature 143

Chapter 11. The Devil in Music 157

Conclusion 169

Index 173

Introduction

The Devil is for some a physical reality, for others a real but purely spiritual person, for some a figment of the imagination and dark fantasy, for yet others a personification of the dark side of the human mind and nature. However he is imagined or understood, he is one of the central figures of theology, literature, and popular culture. We may not believe in him, his existence and power, in the way that our ancestors did and yet he remains a fascinating and absorbing figure, as his role in popular culture attests. One of the reasons why he continues to have such a hold on the imagination and the concept or idea of the Devil has proved to be an enduring one, is because the idea captures something profound in the way we experience the world and our life in it. It helps many to understand or make sense of things that otherwise seem meaningless and terrible.

One of the crucial things to realise is that he is not found all over the world, in all of the many traditions and civilisations. Instead the idea of the Devil is first identified in the old Persian religion of Zoroastrianism and becomes an important element of the three monotheistic faiths – Judaism, Christianity, and Islam. Judaism has now rejected the concept and so the Devil survives as an idea and concept in Christianity and Islam, particularly the former. The intellectual idea of the Devil and the narratives and detailed accounts based on that idea are not found in the classical pagan and polytheistic religions, nor in Hinduism or Buddhism. In these other traditions there are dark gods and goddesses and even demons, forces of destruction and suffering or disorder but these are not the same as the Devil. They are rather part of a larger order, with their own role to play. Often the dark gods and their more benign counterparts are both seen as aspects of a higher totality.

In contrast the Devil has two qualities that distinguish him from the dark deities of the world. He is malevolent, he knowingly and consciously wills the bad (something many philosophers think is impossible but which many artists and ordinary people find both possible and plausible). Moreover, he is the adversary, the enemy of the Good and of its origin, God. He may be more of a sparring partner than a true competitor but that does not make his enmity any less real or intense and above all he is not part of a larger system, an element that has to exist for the system as a whole to work. Rather, he is a force that exists for now but which ultimately will be defeated and destroyed. This vision, of a malevolent spiritual being of immense power, set in implacable enmity to the good and God, is a creation of monotheism, and its formulation and elaboration is one of the most important aspects of the division and separation of the monotheistic faiths from the rest of the world's religions and traditions.

From that something else follows. The idea of the Devil, as we have it now and as it has existed in Christianity and Islam for centuries, has not always been around. It does not exist in the older parts of the Old Testament for example. So, the Devil was in some sense created. The idea of the devil has not always been a part of the mental furniture of human beings, it came into existence in a particular time and place and gradually took form and definition. He was not however invented out of whole cloth, nor was the concept of the Devil, a malevolent spiritual power, one that was created by specific people at a very particular point in time. Rather the idea gradually came together over several centuries, with the various elements combining until they formed a complete and fascinating whole. This was the work of many hands and of a process of dialogue and argument, done in part to meet certain intellectual needs and with particular ends in mind. The process that created the idea of the Devil drew upon older and more universal ideas and beliefs but also added new ones that appeared in a more limited time and place, the Mediterranean world and Middle East of the period from the second century BC to around the fourth century AD. In the process older ideas and images were transformed and something genuinely novel was created, without there being a single and identifiable author. Simultaneously, this process elaborated a narrative, a story of what the Devil was, his nature, how he came to be, and what part he played in the story of the world and of humankind. The narrative drew upon older texts and stories but invested them with truly novel meanings, ones that went on to inspire subsequent artists and writers.

One can argue is that what happened at that time and in that process was not that the Devil was invented or created but that human beings became for the first time conscious or aware of him. They came to realise the truth of his existence and what he was and was doing in a way that they had not been before. In either case there is an origin or starting point to the story of the Devil as an idea and a belief, one with many far-reaching effects. This is not though a story that has only one chapter. Once formed, the idea of Satan, the adversary, the Devil, went on to evolve and acquire new detail as the centuries went by, so that we may fairly speak of a biography of the Devil, as we trace the ways in which the conception that people had of him, and the way he was represented, changed over time. One such change took place in the transition from the world of late antiquity to that of the Middle Ages, another, very dramatic, one happened at the very end of the Middle Ages in the period commonly known as the Renaissance. In more recent times there has been a further shift with the Devil becoming viewed in a more positive light, and latterly with his becoming an object of humour, albeit of a cruel and troubling kind.

This last reflects something that many observers have noted, which is the decline and decay of the kind of strong positive belief in the existence and reality of the Devil that we once had in Western civilisation and its offshoots. Despite that, the idea retains its fascination and has been explored by several of the greatest writers of the modern era. Moreover, as very recent events have shown, accusations that involve Satan and his machinations, even when made in a secular context and by people who claim not to believe in him, still have the capacity to bring about dramatic and often disastrous results. Almost as soon as the idea of the Devil took firm shape, the related idea appeared that he had servants and collaborators. Some were spiritual beings like himself, of a similar nature and sharing his fate. Others were creatures of the supernatural, characters in much of the folklore of the world but now brought into the army of the Evil One. The final piece of that jigsaw was the belief that he also had knowing, deliberate and conscious human collaborators and worshippers, who had committed the ultimate act in evil and treachery and allied themselves with the Adversary, setting themselves in opposition to Good and in the service of pure Evil and malevolence.

This idea, of an (inevitably secret) conspiracy of people who had gone beyond the usual moral failings of mankind to something more profound, in the shape of systematic service of evil and opposition to good, is a recurring dark fantasy of the Western mind it would seem. The result, whenever it has taken hold on the minds of people with power, has been disastrous, in the shape of literal and metaphorical witch-hunts. The fantasy clearly retains its power, and derives from the core element of the belief in the Devil, which remains a part of the mental furniture of contemporary people in many parts of the world, that there can be such a thing as pure malevolence, which explains certain kinds of terrible or cruel acts (and secondarily, that some people are motivated by this to do things). This belief has survived the fading of its instantiation in the notion of an actual person who embodies and creates that malevolence.

All of these ideas have played a huge part in the legal, intellectual, cultural, and social history of the West and increasingly the entire world. You cannot write a history of the last two thousand years in which the Devil does not appear, even if only because you cannot ignore the way people have written about him, portrayed him in the representational arts, or alluded to him in music. Today this is as true as it has ever been from popular music to cinema and television or popular fiction. The Devil is still someone you cannot ignore, even if he has managed to persuade many that he does not exist. How though to make sense of all this, to know why and how he slowly emerged into the consciousness of humanity, how he changed over time, and how people have represented him, referred to him and understood his doings and those of his servants and allies. Fortunately, there is an extensive literature on all of this, from the pens of many scholars over the centuries. In recent years there has been a sudden spurt in writing of this kind, with a wide range of often excellent works appearing in print.

What this Streetwise Guide does is to give a short introduction to the high points of that scholarship so that by reading it one may get a picture of the nature of the Devil, the story of how he became explicitly believed in and thought about and how over time this idea has changed and its aspects and implications have affected the world, particularly the realms of literature, music, and the arts. As it is meant to be an introduction there are short lists of suggested further reading attached to each chapter although these in turn are not comprehensive but rather an indication of the best places to start on the unending activity of finding out more about the Devil and his works.

Suggested Reading
Oldridge, Darren (2012) *The Devil: A Very Short Introduction.* Oxford University Press.

Russell, Jeffrey Burton (1992) *The Prince of Darkness: Radical Evil and the Power of Good in History.* Cornell University Press.

Chapter 1. The Devil: The Basic Idea

Most or all of us have a mental image of the Devil, often taken from the genre of cartoon caricature, a figure with a pitchfork, horns, a tail, and cloven hooves for feet. We know that he lives in Hell or is bound there but he seems to pop up in many other places, so if he is confined, he clearly has a day pass at least. Another part of the image is that he is a tempter and seducer who encourages us to give in to our darker desires or puts suggestions in our minds. Today in Western countries most do not believe in the actual existence of such a being but there are more who still do than one might think. Among those who take the concept seriously some think of him as having an actual physical existence (although that is now rare) while others believe that although an actual person, he is by nature a spiritual and immaterial being or entity. The commonest view of him, particularly among those obliged to think about him in a professional capacity, is that he is a kind of personification or objectification of the dark side of human nature and the human capacity for evil and cruelty. What is striking is how familiar the ideas and images are and how much people know, or believe they know about him even if they do not believe in his existing in some sense. This knowledge though is partial and it pays to elaborate the essential features of the Devil and his main qualities. Who or what is he? What is his nature and where did he come from? What part does he play in the larger story in which he is a character, the Christian and Islamic account of the world?

The fundamental point about him is that he is evil. He is without redeeming quality or virtues, at least as he was originally thought of and imagined. (This changed later, as we shall see). What though is evil? All human beings agree that there is such a thing and can give examples of it. Trying to define it is more difficult and has taxed many of the greatest minds. That does not stop most people from being sure of its existence and certain that they know what it is, even if they can't put that understanding into words. To paraphrase a US Supreme Court Justice, we may not be able to say what it is but we know it when we see it. The common element to most descriptions is suffering. Evil is the part of life that involves pain, loss, and deprivation. That however is only the start of the challenge of definition. In practice most people who have thought about the problem of evil have concluded that there are two kinds of category of things that we can attach that label to. The first is that of what we may call natural evil, the suffering, pain and loss that results from features of the natural world such as disasters and catastrophic events, age and illness, or accidents. For some this would include things such as the suffering and pain that is part of nature, as in the relations between predator and prey or host and parasite for example. Evil in that sense is pervasive and inescapable. It is also natural in a very specific sense: it does not derive from human beings or their actions and choices (rather it is something that happens to them) and as such it is not the product of willed choice (at least, not in the common contemporary view). However, there is a second category of evil. That is the bad things, the pain, suffering and loss that result from human choice and which has therefore been willed by human beings (in the sense that a human being had to act purposefully for it to happen, so it was brought about by an act of will, will being the active part of the mind).

This leads in turn to another distinction. In many cases (most philosophers would say all) the people whose choices bring about the evil do not intend that choice knowing that it will result in evil and doing it for that reason, precisely to bring about that evil. Instead, they will or intend something else without realising that doing so will bring about evil or they know it will bring about evil but believe that will be necessary for something good to happen, which will outweigh the bad. In some instances however, we have what seems to most people to be radical evil, the bringing about of bad things deliberately and as an end in itself. What we have here is acts that are motivated not through following a misguided understanding of the good or because doing them will ultimately lead to a better end but rather by pure spite and malice. This is how we often understand gratuitous cruelty and sadism where the cruelty has no obvious or necessary connection to any goal or purpose, however misguided: it is an end in itself. This radical evil, pure malice, is not part of the natural or non-human world most of us now believe. Rather, it is distinctively human. If so where does it come from, and what does it say about us as a type of being, and our nature? This is where the Devil comes in. Before he was invented or discovered the common practice was to make no distinction between the human world and the natural, in this or in other respects. Humans were part of a natural world and qualities that they had were shared by the rest of the natural order, including the capacity to cause evil. What appeared was a way of thinking where humans were seen as separate from the natural world but this made the question of why radical evil existed more acute. The answer was that there was a being or entity who caused it.

The second feature of the Devil as a concept is that he is an entity, of immense power and ability to affect the world. Because his power is so universal and profound, he must be a spiritual being, even if he also has a physical nature, because only a being that was spiritual and not limited by the constraints of time and matter could have such extraordinary power and capacity. He is the cause of evil, the reason why it exists, for some only in the human world, for many in both the human and natural worlds. This makes evil problematic and, in a sense, unnatural: it is something that should not exist (as opposed to being regrettable but inevitable). The Devil is the explanation for this, the cause of it. He is an entity or being or force precisely because he has a will. It is his actions and choices that result in and bring about evil and suffering. If not then he would be a part of the world and evil would also be a part of that order. The concept means that as a spiritual entity he is active in the world we know and experience and has an effect on it but he is also not a part of it, even though he exists within it and operates upon it. He has come from elsewhere and probably predates it, he is an outside force that marrs or distorts the world but is not himself a part of it.

The fact of his having a will is to say that he has the capacity for choice, reflection, and understanding: he is not an automaton or creature that is guided by instinct and can do only what he does. He chooses or wills what he does. This brings us to the third and central quality of the Devil. He is malevolent. That is, he consciously, knowingly, and deliberately wills the bad. He has an evil will. He is in some sense a personification or embodiment of pure unadulterated spite and malice. For a whole tradition of philosophy from Plato onwards the idea of malevolence is at least problematic and more likely nonsense or incoherent. For Plato and those who agree with him, it is impossible to be truly malevolent. That is because in this way of thinking evil as a quality has no positive actual existence of its own; it is only the radical weakening or absence of the good. Since one cannot will a negative or absence it follows that we cannot actually will or chose evil: what we do is to will a mistaken notion of the good or an incorrect means of realising it. The contrary view is that even if we grant the argument that evil is only the absence or destruction of the good it is still possible to be malevolent because we can imagine someone who hates the good precisely because it is good and wishes and wills its destruction. This is malevolence. Interestingly, many of the most arresting expressions of this view come from authors who have portrayed malevolent characters or actions that are purely malevolent in their motivation. William Shakespeare is one of the best examples as several of his most memorable and powerful characters are malevolent – Iago, Richard III, Aaron the Moor to give just three examples. Another directly relevant example is that of Satan in Milton's *Paradise Lost*, with Milton using his soliloquies to explore the nature of malevolent motivation. Most readers find such portrayals persuasive and plausible, which suggests that as far as human experience goes Plato was missing something. There is a rival tradition in philosophy that asserts both the existence of evil and the need for the concept to understand or categorise certain kinds of action and choice. Believing in the possibility of evil and malevolence does not mean that one therefore has to believe in the Devil, a malevolent power who is the source of evil, but it does make that belief possible. Moreover, the formulation of the idea of a malevolent being was a key part of the origins of both the separation between human action and natural action and also the problematisation of evil as something produced by the choice of acting agents.

All accounts of the Devil have these two features, that he is a spiritual being or force and that he is malevolent. At this point though ideas about his nature diverge and from the beginning there are three different views of his nature and existence. The orthodox view is that he is an actual person, a being with a personal identity. This is similar to the Christian conception of Jesus, who as the Son is God but also a distinct person, one of the three persons of the trinity. So in this way of thinking, which is the predominant one among both Christians and Muslims for most of history, the Devil, (Satan or Iblis) is an actual individual being and person in the same way as you or I even if he is spiritual rather than physical – he is immensely more powerful and also immortal but he is not different in his nature and he exists as an actual person with a name, an identity and a history or biography. It is because he is a person that we can speak of his having a will and a purpose. A different way of understanding him, which has become widespread in more recent times, is that he is an entity but not a person in the usual understanding of the term. According to this he is not a person but a personification, of the dark side of human nature and the human mind. In this way of thinking it is each of us who may sometimes display malevolence and knowingly will the bad.

The malevolent will is a feature or quality of all human beings, at least potentially, even if it is not always realised. What personification of this dark part of our nature, thinking of it as a separate thing, does is to make that reality both more solid and at the same time easier to grasp or understand. It also fits in to the idea that we must resist or deny and control this aspect of our being, which otherwise can break free and come to dominate our will and decisions, with disastrous results. There is a third position, which combines the first two. According to this, the Devil is a person or being but he exists within our minds or works through us and our actions and choices. This can be combined with the idea of the collective unconscious, the notion of a kind of shared group mind at the unconscious and unarticulated level, something that is common to all human beings and can act both through particular individuals and large groups or even the entire population of the world. The Devil is then the dark side or Shadow of that collective subconscious, the force within not only each mind and self but the collective totality of all human minds that wills or desires destructiveness and hate.

The fourth essential feature of the Devil is that he does not exist on his own but in opposition to God, in fact it is that that defines what he is (in the same way that for thinkers who follow Plato evil can only be defined in contrast or opposition to good). He is the adversary, the enemy of God, his opponent throughout all times and in all places and in the hearts and minds of all human beings everywhere and in every age. He seeks constantly to subvert God's purpose and to defeat it, this is his only goal. Himself forever damned and cast out by God, he seeks constantly to corrupt the divine creation and to seduce others so that they share in his damnation. Given that he appears mainly in monotheistic religions this raises obvious challenges, which have taxed the wits and intellects of theologians and apologists for centuries.

The obvious problem is this: if he is the adversary of God and his opponent then whence comes his power – how is he able to do this, and why? This is not a problem in the first religious tradition to formulate the idea of an eternal malevolent power, the old Persian religion of Zoroastrianism. There the Good Lord and the Dark

Lord are equal and coeval powers matched against each other in conflict but each with their own power. In the three monotheistic faiths this does not apply, as in all of them God is omnipotent (all powerful) which logically means that if the Devil has power and works against God then it is God Himself who has given him that power and allows him to do this. Two questions follow from this. The first is how to make sense of this, if we can. The other is to ask why then the three monotheistic faiths at one time all shared the idea of a malevolent adversary to God and his will. If that notion causes such intellectual difficulty then why have it?

The answer is that it is difficult for monotheistic religions to do without some notion of an adversary because it helps to deal with what is otherwise a huge challenge to the monotheistic way of thinking. This is the problem of divine justice or theodicy, which arises because of the way all three faiths attribute two qualities to God: he is all powerful (omnipotent) and he is perfectly good and always and only wills the good (he is omnibenevolent). The difficulty is how to reconcile these given the undeniable existence of suffering, and even more troublingly, of deliberate cruelty and malice. How can the existence of these things be made compatible with God being both all-powerful and perfectly good? This is also connected to the fact that in the monotheistic faiths God is transcendent – he is not a part of the world because the world derives its existence from him and he existed before it and beyond it. This is because if the universe has an existence independent of and prior to God's will then he is not omnipotent. (This is radically different from the divine powers of other traditions who order the world and govern it but are also part of it and in which the universe existed before the gods and independently of them – they shape and guide it but do not create it). This means that God, the divine power, has created the world (and even, in orthodox Islamic theology, continues constantly to recreate it at every instant of time). If that is so, then why if he is all good, did he create a world with suffering and evil? And why does he allow it to continue?

There are several possible answers to that challenge which, however, are incompatible with the monotheistic faiths. One is to say that he could have created a perfect world and could end evil but chooses not to. This means that he is not benevolent, indeed in the extreme case it means he is actually malevolent so that we live in a world created by an evil power that does not wish us well (this is the view of Gnosticism). Another possibility is that he is benevolent and wished to create a perfect world and wishes to eliminate suffering and evil but is unable to do so or is incompetent. In that case he is not omnipotent. It could be that he neither wishes to eliminate evil nor is he able to do so but, in that case, he is not God. There are only two ways to resolve this and save the combination of omnipotence and omnibenevolence. The first is the one that Judaism eventually arrived at and which many Muslim theologians advocate. That is that God is indeed responsible for all of the suffering and evil in the world and he does permit it or even cause it but that we have to simply accept it. We do not know what God knows and we do not understand the purpose or nature of his actions. It is not for us to question them; we must simply accept them. This response, of strict monotheism and fatalism, is expressed in the closing passage of the biblical *Book of Job*, when God speaks to Job and his comforters out of a whirlwind and castigates them for their presumptuousness. This position is consistent but for many people deeply unsatisfying. Consequently, they turn to the alternative escape route, which is to have an adversary.

In this way of thinking God created a world that was initially perfect but he also created an adversary or challenger, whom he allows both freedom of will and the ability to strive against him. The adversary seeks to mar and damage or even destroy God's work and to thwart and corrupt his purpose. In this scenario the adversary is something like a sparring partner because he cannot ultimately triumph (since clearly that would deny God's omnipotence). However, the adversary does have a will of his own, he is not simply a puppet. He strives constantly to do as much damage as he can and will do so as long as he is allowed to. Why though create and allow such a power? What is the point of it? Several answers have been given to that question, of why God allows the Devil freedom of will and action. One, which relates to his origins as we shall see in the next chapter, is that he is a tester whose task is to test and examine the faith and virtue of another part of the divine creation, humanity. The commonest answer though is that he is a necessary part of the creation and by existing and doing what he does he plays a part in God's ultimate design. The argument is that evil is necessary to perfect the good and raise it to its highest level, that evil makes possible higher forms of good and virtue that would not exist in its absence. The Devil is thus a hostile power who brings out and makes possible a stronger and fuller kind of good. This still does not satisfy many people but it does answer the challenge of theodicy without resorting to fatalism or denying free will.

This brings us to another key feature of the Devil. Although he is immortal, he has not always been as he is now. Since he was created by God, he was not evil from the beginning (since that would also limit God's goodness). Therefore, he is fallen from his initial state, as humanity is. The critical difference in that regard is that in the human case our wills are corrupted so that even though we will the good we do not do it but rather do the evil that we do not will (as St Paul says) whereas the Devil as a spiritual being has a perfect will and having once fallen can never repent or regret. Because he is fallen there must have been an event or occasion that brought that about. For Christians this was when as Lucifer he rebelled against God and took with him a third part of the Heavenly host. For Muslims it was when Iblis, one of the spiritual powers created by Allah, disobeyed him and refused to bow to the newly created Adam. In both cases it is an act of defiance or rebellion against God's will that is the central act. In addition, although he presently wages war on God he will not always be able to do so, at some point his career will be ended and he will either be destroyed, or bound and rendered powerless for eternity. He may be powerful and pervasive at present but at some point in the future there will be a last climactic struggle in which he will be definitively defeated. This all means that he is a part of history and plays a central role in a narrative arc that includes the creation of the world, the temptation and fall of Adam and Eve, the ministry, death, and resurrection of Jesus (for Christians) and the ministry and revelation of the Prophet Muhammad (for Muslims) and, in the future, the apocalypse or unveiling of God's purpose at the end of things as they are. So, he is bound into and part of a larger story with a beginning central event and end. This conception of historical time as having a beginning, middle, and end is also peculiar to the monotheistic faiths and Zoroastrianism, as the world's other traditions mostly adhere to a cyclical view of time and existence.

The Devil being a creation of God or licensed by Him, and acting within this world for as long as it exists, is the reason for another important feature of the idea of the Adversary. Although he is powerful, he is not omnipotent (as that quality pertains only to God). One aspect of this is that he cannot work true miracles (a miracle is, by definition, a suspension of the laws of nature or the production of an act or event that violates those laws). He may seem to do so or enable his servants to do so but these are tricks and illusions. It is only God who can work miracles, either directly or through an agent such as a saint or Prophet. The Devil can only act within the laws of nature. However, because his knowledge is so much greater than ours, he can do things and bring about results that seem miraculous to us. He can also give knowledge and hence power to his servants and devotees. One aspect of this is the belief that there is a body of lore or knowledge about how we may do this and use the Devil's knowledge of and ability to act upon the world through the laws of nature and it is this that accounts for the close association in both Western and Islamic thought between the Devil and ritual magic of all kinds. It also explains the historically close connection between the occult and magic on the one hand and science on the other, and the way that in the modern world there has been a persistent current of thought in both popular and elite culture that connects Lucifer with reason and enlightenment and the ways of modern science.

One area where there is disagreement is over how far the Devil can act directly in this world through physical means. In the Ancient and Medieval worlds, it was widely thought that he could and he was held accountable for things such as natural disasters, plagues and famines. This reflected the ultimate origins of the idea of Satan, as we shall see. As time passed this idea came to have less force and was largely (though not entirely) supplanted by another. This is the notion that the Devil cannot act directly in the physical world but must do so through human agents. Some are deliberate and conscious agents of his will, a persistent belief that repeatedly has disastrous results. More often though he acts by tempting or misleading people, by manipulating them and perverting their will and intentions so that they act in ways that serve the Devil without realising it – at least initially. This is yet another central part of the idea of the Devil, for both Christians and Muslims. The Devil is a tempter or corrupter and seducer, who leads men and women astray and seeks always to turn them against God and his purpose so that they will work to corrupt or destroy and damage what is good. He will use all kinds of methods and features of the human mind and will to do this

The Devil also has certain qualities which are reflected in the epithets and titles that are attached to him, and he has a whole series of associations, particularly in Christian thinking. He is a lord, the ruler of Hell and legions of dark spirits and other beings, like himself but of less power. He has an array of servants and collaborators. As such he is the Dark Lord, the Prince of Darkness and even the ruler of this world – at least for now. He is the Tempter and corrupter, the Evil One, the Father of Lies. He has many names, Lucifer, Satan, and Iblis being the most commonly used but he is also identified with Mephistopheles, Beelzebub, Belial, Baal, and Asmodeus (though most see these as the names of some of his subordinates). In the modern world and popular vernacular he has acquired a range of nicknames, such as Old Nick or Old Scratch. There is a long list of things that he is associated with. The best known is the dragon (derived from an explicit connection made in *Revelations*) but he is also identified with snakes and in particular with the Serpent in *Genesis*. There are a number of other animals that are linked to him, such as the donkey (because of its association with lust) and the goat (because of the passage in *St Matthew's Gospel* where the damned are the goats), the pig (because of its being an unclean and prohibited animal for Jews and Muslims), and also toads and frogs. He is associated with salt water and with certain natural phenomena, most obviously night and darkness but also the desert and extreme weather events. In particular he is associated with extremes of both heat and cold. He is left-handed and associated with the left as opposed to the right (hence the double meaning of 'sinister') and the system of magic that is connected to him is known as the 'left hand path'. His colour is black but he is also associated with red and is often portrayed as wearing red clothes. He even has an ascribed coat of arms, deduced from a passage in Revelations. The details of his appearance in the popular imagination have varied and changed over time, as we shall see, but have also remained constant over long spans of time, so that we may speak in that sense of a medieval, renaissance and modern devil.

The Devil is envisaged as resident in a specific location, which is Hell, thought of as being both his place of imprisonment and punishment and his domain where he carries out one of his functions, of tormenting and punishing the unfortunate souls he has ensnared and led astray. The details of Hell again have changed over time as we shall see in Chapter 6, and in particular there was a dramatic shift in the way the notion of Hell was understood around the time of the Renaissance. At the same time, he is active and present throughout the world, walking up and down and travelling through the world. He can also be summoned or brought to mind by speaking his name, or thinking of him, or indulging in sin although there is a more elaborated theory of how he and his associates can be invoked and made to appear in physical form by employing certain techniques and practices. This tension, between his being physically located and confined in a particular place, and simultaneously being active and present in the world is explained by his spiritual nature which enables his will and actions to transcend the limits of time and space, even if he is also thought of as having an actual physical body (which increasingly he is not).

The Devil then, is a complex idea or notion with a number of central elements that constitute his nature and role, as well as other adventitious attributes that shift and change over time. As explained at the start though, this concept, of a malevolent and destructive spiritual being of immense power, who is the adversary of God and the good and engaged in unending struggle against them, and so being one of the driving forces in history, is not something that has always existed. For thousands of years in the ancient world and to this day in the indigenous cultures of South and East Asia, human beings have managed without him or the idea of him and have thought about the world and time in ways that do not require such an idea or entity. By contrast since the idea came into existence an ever larger part of the world has had the idea of the Devil as a key part of their mental furniture, with a huge influence on how they think about and understand such things as good and evil, human action and motivation, and the structure and meaning of history and much of the natural world. We may flatter ourselves that today we have escaped from this but in fact in this as in other ways our patterns of thought and intellectual categories are still shaped by the ideas of monotheism, of which the Devil is a major one. How though and when and where did this idea come into existence?

Further Reading

In addition to the works by Oldridge and Russell cited after the introduction, the following are general surveys of the idea and of the Devil and his historical development.

Almond, Philip C. 2016. *The Devil: A New Biography.* I.B. Tauris.

Carus, Paul (2008, 1st published 1900) *The History of the Devil and the Idea of Evil, From the Earliest Times to the Present Day.* Dover.

Chignell, Andrew P. (2019) *Evil: A History*. Oxford University Press.

Gosden, Chris (2020) *The History of Magic: from Alchemy to Witchcraft, from the Ice Age to the Present.* Penguin.

Graham, Gordon (2000) *Evil and Christian Ethics*. Cambridge University Press.

Maxwell-Stuart, P. G. (2008) *Satan: A Biography*. Tempus.

Medway, Gareth J. (2001) *Lure of the Sinister: The Unnatural History of Satanism.* New York University Press.

Messadie, Gerald (1997) *A History of the Devil*. Kodansha International Press.

Morgan, Genevieve & Tom (1996). *The Devil: A Visual Guide to the Demonic, Evil, Scurrilous, and Bad.* Chronicle Books.

Muchembled, Robert (2003). *A History of the Devil from the Middle Ages to the Present.* Polity Press.

Muchembled, Robert (2004) *Damned: An Illustrated History of the Devil.* Editions du Seuil.

Russell, Jeffry Burton (1977) *The Devil: Perceptions of Evil from Antiquity to Primitive Christianity.* Cornell University Press.

Stanford, Peter (1996) *The Devil: A Biography*. Heinemann.

Wilson, Amelia (2002) *The Devil*. Barrons.

The Devil's attributed coat of arms (from Wikimedia Commons).

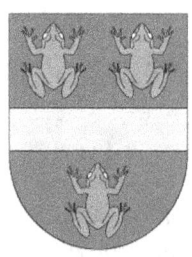

Chapter 2. The Origins of the Devil

The traditional religious traditions of the world have many examples of what we may call 'dark' gods and goddesses. These are divine beings who are associated with and responsible for features of the natural world that humans find threatening, disagreeable or terrifying. The gods may be thought of as the personifications of those phenomena. Some are the embodiment of chaos, of the old order or rather disorder that the gods had put down and arranged so as to make human life possible. One prominent example of this is the Mesopotamian goddess Tiamat, who represents chaos and the infertile waters of the sea. Most dark deities however are associated with features of the natural and human world, but ones that people associate with suffering or loss. Despite their associations they often occupy prominent places in the pantheons of traditional or pagan religious traditions. The most obvious of these is the god or goddess of death and the afterlife, which is usually seen as dull and gloomy, for most at least. Others are the deities of sickness, of natural disasters such as storm, earthquake, drought, plague and famine and also of human wrongdoing such as war and violence. One example is the Egyptian god Set, the personification of the desert and drought, another is the Egyptian lion-headed goddess Sekhmet who personifies the destructive aspect of the sun and also war and anger. On the other side of the world this description fits many of the deities of the Mesoamerican and Andean religions, such as Tezcatlipoca, the Smoking Mirror, the god of plague and natural disaster in the pantheons of Middle America. He is also though the god of beauty, human intelligence, and rulership and this ambivalence is characteristic of the dark gods and goddesses of the various pagan traditions.

For the main point about the dark gods of traditional paganism is that while they may be fearful or threatening, they are not malevolent. They are rather a part of the natural and divine order. Often, they have qualities that are usually seen as admirable, alongside their other ones. Thus, Hades, the god of death and the afterlife in classical Greek paganism, is certainly implacable and inescapable, grim and unsympathetic, but he is also just, impartial and honourable. The point is that, however unpleasant their deeds may be for humans, such dark divinities are natural and not motivated by malice or hatred of the good – they are not about destruction or corruption for its own sake. We might say that in bringing calamities and things such as death upon mankind they are simply doing their job, as such things are a part of the natural order, which we have to accept along with the good. Moreover, in the traditional religions all of the deities are to our way of thinking morally ambiguous. The gods bring both good and bad, often in a capricious and unpredictable fashion. Thus Apollo, the god of reason and light, is also the god of plague and epidemic illness. If there are dark but not malevolent gods, traditional religions have few if any deities that are simply and purely good. This kind of moral ambivalence may be a more accurate reflection of the actual world but to those brought up in a culture influenced by the monotheistic faiths it seems strange.

What is notable is that the God of the Old Testament, Yahweh, is one of those ambivalent figures. As any reading of the Bible will reveal, he does things that are hard to reconcile with the idea of a purely good God, as he is responsible for and sometimes even directly orders things that strike us as abhorrent. In the *Book of Joshua*, the Israelites are commanded to slay all of the inhabitants of the land of Canaan without mercy, man, woman, and child. When, after the period of divinely ordained ethnic cleansing, they allow some to live God is enraged and punishes them. Later on, we are told how he tempted David to conduct a census and then punished the Israelites for doing this, even though he was ultimately responsible (the reason was to demonstrate who was boss). Clearly, in the period when the earlier writings of the Old Testament were put together Yahweh was seen as the author of all that happened whether good or bad, and as being as capricious as one of the Greek deities. This however would change later. One important feature of the way he is portrayed is that, like a monarch, he has a court with many subordinates who carry out his will and put it into effect. Thus, plagues are brought by angels (messengers or agents) of the Lord. One particular angel, Sammael, is the angel of death and destruction. Another angelic servant was to change in important ways, and ultimately transform into Satan, the adversary.

The problem or challenge, of having divine powers that were responsible for both good and bad features of both the world and human action, could be dealt with in several ways as religion became more abstract and philosophical during the so-called axial age (between the eighth and third centuries BC). One way, which became predominant in Hinduism and is also found in Buddhism, is monism. According to this there is one single reality, produced by a supreme being, which unites both light and darkness, good and evil and reconciles them in a higher (or alternatively more profound and fundamental) level of reality. The contrast between good and evil is therefore an illusion, produced by our lack of full understanding. The supreme being is beyond such categories. This way of thinking can also be found in the monotheistic faiths, particularly later Judaism but also in Islam. The other response is to make the gods as a whole less ambivalent and to distinguish more clearly between the gods of light and those of darkness. The latter are increasingly thought of as inimical or hostile to humanity and consequently are not worshipped or venerated in the same way – this is what happens with Set for example. However, they are still not thought of as being truly evil or malevolent, it is just that they represent that part of the world that is hostile or dangerous to humanity.

This approach was particularly prevalent in the Middle East, possibly because the harsh and unstable nature of the natural environment there made people unusually aware of the dark side of nature. It was in that part of the world that the process was taken a stage further and the idea of a truly malevolent or destructive divine power came into being. This happened in Persia, in the shape of the traditional religion of Iran, Zoroastrianism (which survives today mainly in India, in the Parsee community). It was founded by the prophet Zoroaster, who is traditionally supposed to have lived during the sixth century BC (and so during the aforementioned axial age). The central belief of Zoroastrianism is dualism. This is the belief that there are two opposed, equal, and coeval divine powers that are in conflict with one another. One, Ahura Mazda or Ormuzd, is the Good God, the creator of all that is good and beneficent and the source of both order and virtue. The other, Angra Mainyu or Ahriman, is the Dark God, the source of evil, decay, destruction and all that is bad. The two are opposed and in continual conflict both in the world and within the thoughts and mind of every person. The key opposition is between Asha meaning truth and virtue, and Druj, meaning falsehood and deceit. (For Zoroastrians and ancient Persians, the lie was the source of evil since it denied or perverted what was). Both Ormuzd and Ahriman have servants or agents, for Ormuzd the seven Amesha Spentas and for Ahriman the Daevas. The person of Ahriman is the first we know of who is truly malevolent and negative, not a part of the benign and original creation. (Also interestingly, given later developments in both Judaism and Christianity, it appears that in the original teachings of Zoroaster Angra Mainyu is evil or perverted thought rather than an actual entity).

The ancient Hebrews came into contact with Zoroastrianism in the aftermath of the Babylonian Captivity, when they were subjects of the Achaemenid Persian Empire (with its founder Cyrus the Great returning them to the Holy Land). This had a major impact upon the Jewish faith, as did internal developments, during what is known as the Second Temple period of Jewish history, between the return from Babylon and the destruction of the Temple in 70 AD. Particularly in the latter part of that period there were a number of developments in Jewish thought, many of which only survive in apocryphal texts produced at that time, such as the *Book of Enoch* or the *Book of Jubilees*. One important part of this was the increasing focus upon and interest in the figure of the Messiah, hence the name given to the thought of the period by many scholars, messianic Judaism. There was in addition another aspect, which was a transformation in the understanding of one of the servants of Yahweh and members of his court. This was satan, or, as he was called initially, *the* satan (making it clear that this was an epiphet or role as much as a person). The transformation of his nature and identity shows how the problem of evil was addressed not through monism nor by going all the way to a full-blown dualism but by a kind of compromise and the creation of an adversary, subordinate but independent.

In the older books of the Old Testament the word satan is used in several places. Here it usually means an obstruction or agent that obstructs, preventing people from doing something or doing what they either want or ought to do. Thus, in the book of Exodus God prevents Balaam from completing a journey and the text says that he barred his way with a satan (translated as meaning that an angel was sent to obstruct him). The term is also used to mean 'accuser' and in that sense it is attached to an angel or servant of God, a member of the divine court. Sometimes the term seems to refer to a class or type of entity but in the *Book of Job*, and in *Zecariah* it refers to an entity, a specific person who is a servant of God. In both of these cases the satan is something like the Roman Catholic idea of the Devil's Advocate, a person whose role is to accuse people to God for their misdeeds or failings. At the same time the idea grows that the accuser is also the tempter, a being responsible to God whose role is to go around the world tempting people and trying to lead them astray so as to test their faith and obedience to God (an idea that survives in one of the lines of the Lord's Prayer). Satan is thus both the instigator or stirrer up of wrong doing and also the one who reports it to God and lays the accusation before him. At the same time the other meaning of the term persists so that he is also seen as the obstacle, the force or agency that prevents people from obeying God and turns them from the right path. In this he seems to be one of the ambivalent servants of the Lord, like Sammael, who expresses the dark side of the creation.

However, during the Second Temple period the person and conception of Satan became more and more that of a deliberate and conscious obstructor of God's will and therefore an adversary figure. As such he came to take on the features and qualities of Ahriman and became the opponent and enemy of God, working against him and to obstruct him. However, this development did not extend to making him an equal or independent power, he remained always subordinate and took on the role or function of a sparring partner or licensed challenger. This kind of development can be seen most clearly in the non-canonical apocryphal works that were produced in large quantities during this period.

One of these introduced another key ingredient or idea that would be incorporated into the Christian idea of the Devil. The work in question was the *Book of Enoch*. Enoch is one of the antediluvian patriarchs, mentioned briefly and obscurely in the *Book of Genesis* "*And Enoch walked with God and he was not: for God had taken him*" (*Genesis* 5:24). He was however the subject of much storytelling in the rabbinical lore and narratives of Judaism at this time and in these the single line above was explained and expanded. The story was that Enoch had been assumed bodily into heaven and then given a guided tour by an angel. Part of this involved an explanation of how and why the world had come to be so corrupt that God was obliged to cleanse it with the Flood. This in turn involved a story that also glossed or explained another obscure passage in Genesis "*that the sons of God saw the daughters of men that they were fair; and they took them wives of all which they chose. And the Lord said, My spirit shall not always strive with man, for that he also is flesh: yet his days shall be an hundred and twenty years. There were giants in the earth in those days; and also after that, when the sons of God* came in unto the daughters of men, and they bare children to them, the same became mighty men which were of old, men of renown" (*Genesis* 6: 1–4). The story in *The Book of Enoch* that explained and elaborated this was that of the Watchers.

According to this, after the creation and the expulsion of Adam and Eve from Eden, God sent angels to watch over their descendants, the antediluvian humans (hence Watchers). However, some of these angels lusted after human women and rebelled against their divine commission, descending to earth and having intercourse with human women. Their offspring were the Nephilim, a race of giants. They also taught a whole range of arts and skills and technologies to human beings, knowledge that they were not intended to have or at least not all at once. There are obvious similarities to the Greek myth of Prometheus and his stealing fire from the gods to give to humanity, for which he was bound to a mountain and condemned to have his liver consumed daily by an eagle. In Genesis the skills and arts that the Watchers taught are also associated with the children and descendants of Cain, the first murderer.

The text in *Enoch* that describes the rebellion of the Watchers reads as follows: "*And it came to pass when the children of men had multiplied that in those days were born unto them beautiful and comely daughters. And the angels, the children of the heaven, saw and lusted after them, and said to one another: "Come, let us choose us wives from among the children of men and beget us children." And Semjaza, who was their leader, said unto them: "I fear ye will not indeed agree to do this deed, and I alone shall have to pay the penalty of a great sin." And they all answered him and said: "Let us all swear an oath, and all bind ourselves by mutual imprecations not to abandon this plan but to do this thing." Then sware they all together and bound themselves by mutual imprecations upon it. And they were in all two hundred; who descended in the days of Jared on the summit of Mount Hermon, and they called it Mount Hermon, because they had sworn and bound themselves by mutual imprecations upon it* "(*Enoch* 1: 6–11). God then sent the Flood to destroy the Nephilim, and the human beings that the Watchers had misled. According to the *Book of Enoch* the Watchers are bound 'in the valleys of the Earth' until the Day of Judgment. This is alluded to in the New Testament *Epistle of Jude*, which contains the line "*And the angels which kept not their first estate, but left their own habitation, he hath reserved in everlasting chains under darkness unto the judgment of the great day.*" (*Jude* 1:6).

This myth or narrative has been rejected or radically reinterpreted by later orthodox Judaism and most Christian theology but it was a widespread idea during the first century BC. What it introduced was the idea of a rebellion among the angels who served God, by which they fell from their position and either came down to Earth or were cast down there, and by which act of rebellion, sin and disobedience to God entered the world. What this means is that by the last century BC there was a widespread form of messianic Judaism that contained two key ideas. Firstly, that among the supernatural powers or angels was one, Satan, the accuser or obstructor, who was increasingly seen as the tempter of humanity and the adversary of God, and secondly the idea of a rebellion among the angelic heavenly host, that had brought wickedness but also knowledge and civilisation into the world. These two ideas were initially distinct but connected by the fact of the Watchers being identified in the text as satans, that is obstructors of God's will. In addition, an obscure part of the Enochian texts implied that the Watchers followed a previous rebellion by another angel, Azazel. This was a part of the milieu in which Christianity took shape.

In the texts that were eventually brought together to form the Christian canon and so the New Testament (which were only a small part of the many works circulating in the first three centuries AD) the figure of the adversary plays a more prominent role than in most of the Old Testament. In the Greek translations of these works the term used to describe him is the Greek *diabolos,* which we now render as the Devil. In the Gospels the Devil appears as the one who obstructs and hinders Gods work (as for example in the parable of the sower). He is also clearly one of many, as several of the miracles of Jesus involve the expulsion and casting out of devils (as opposed to the singular one who takes the definite article). Most notably in the passage where Jesus following his fast in the wilderness is tempted by the Devil, he is clearly meant to be an enemy and opponent of God and Jesus addresses him as Satan, making that a proper personal name. So, the early Christian writings have the idea of the Devil as an adversary, the great opponent of God and as such the antagonist of Jesus. This kind of thinking, which clearly reflects the development of Jewish beliefs as found in texts like the *Book of Jubilees*, is also shown by the frequent references to the Devil in the epistles, particularly the Pauline ones. Here the emphasis is on the world as a scene of combat between the forces of good and evil, light and darkness, with the Devil the leader of one side. During the second and third centuries AD further developments took place that combined this idea with that of rebellious angels and through reinterpretation of certain key Biblical texts consolidated the idea of the Devil and gave him a leading role in the Christian narrative of the world, the Fall, and Salvation.

During the period of Christian history before the establishment of a definite canon there were many different texts that were read and used by the early Christians in addition to the ones that finally made the 'cut'. Many of these were apocalypses, accounts of the ending of the world, the overthrow and destruction of things as they are and the unveiling or making clear of God's purpose (the word apocalypse means 'unveiling'). Only one of these survived to be accepted as canonical: this was of course the *Revelations of St John*, the final book of the standard Bible as it was ultimately established. The text probably survived because it was traditionally associated with the Apostle John whereas other apocalyptic texts, even when assigned to similar figures, such as the Apostle Peter, were not as widely thought to be genuine.

The aspect or part of the vision narrative of Revelations that concerns us here is firstly the following passage "*And there was war in heaven: Michael and his angels fought against the dragon; and the dragon fought and his angels, And prevailed not; neither was their place found any more in heaven. And the great dragon was cast out, that old serpent, called the Devil, and Satan, which deceiveth the whole world: he was cast out into the earth, and his angels were cast out with him. And I heard a loud voice saying in heaven, Now is come salvation, and strength, and the kingdom of our God, and the power of his Christ: for the accuser of our brethren is cast down, which accused them before our God day and night.*" (*Revelations* 12: 7-10). This passage was widely understood as meaning two things. Firstly, that the Devil was the leader of a revolt in Heaven against God (so incorporating the idea of rebel angels from the myth of the Watchers) that been defeated, after which he and his followers were cast out of Heaven and into the world. The idea was now that Satan, the accuser and obstructor was also the leader of a rebellion and consequently a fallen angel, cast out of God's presence but for a while allowed free reign on Earth. The second conclusion was the identification of Satan with the dragon or serpent – this seems to have been the incorporation of an idea taken from the older Mesopotamian accounts of the way the god Marduk had defeated the goddess

Tiamat, which had passed into the apocalyptic literature of later messianic Judaism.

This in turn led to a reinterpretation or glossing of some key passages in the Bible, which gave Satan a defined nature and biography. The identification of Satan with the serpent led to reinterpretation of the account of the temptation of Eve in Eden. In its original (and clear) meaning the text does not imply that the Serpent was anything other than a part of the creation, it was simply an intelligent and subtle (i.e. sophistical and logic chopping) creature. What happened with the reception of the text of Revelations was that the Serpent was now identified with the fallen angel Satan, who thus became the agent and cause of the temptation and fall of Adam and Eve and the marring and corruption of God's initial creation. The question then was when the initial rebellion of Satan had happened but it was now generally put back to the time of the creation or before it (so unlike the Enochian account of the Watchers in that regard).

This narrative was then supplemented by a reinterpretation of a passage in the Book of Isaiah. *"How you are fallen from heaven, O Lucifer, son of the morning How you are cut down to the ground, You who weakened the nations! For you have said in your heart: 'I will ascend into heaven, I will exalt my throne above the stars of God; I will also sit on the mount of the congregation On the farthest sides of the north; I will ascend above the heights of the clouds, I will be like the Most High.' Yet you shall be brought down to Sheol, To the lowest depths of the Pit. "Those who see you will gaze at you, And consider you, saying: 'Is this the man who made the earth tremble, Who shook kingdoms, Who made the world as a wilderness And destroyed its cities Who did not open the house of his prisoners?"* (Isaiah 14: 12–17).

The original text referred to the King of Babylon, who was likened in the first verse to the morning star (lucifer in Latin). The new interpretation made this an account of Satan's rebellion, defeat, and fall and gave him the name he had born before his expulsion, Lucifer, now made a proper noun. This reading of the text also gave a reason for the rebellion and war in heaven, it was an attempt on the part of one of the greatest of angels to overthrow and supplant God, motivated by pride and denial of the divine order and rebellion against it in a supreme act of self-assertion and hubris. The text was now linked to one in *Luke's Gospel* where Jesus says to his disciples *"And I saw Satan like lightning fall from heaven"* (*Luke* 10: 18). Thus, the Devil against whom he contends and who tempts him unsuccessfully in the wilderness is the same being who brought about the Fall and is a rebel angel, in opposition to God, defeated and yet striving constantly to obstruct him and pervert his creation, above all humanity.

The *Book of Revelation* added the final parts to this narrative and contributed again to the firming up and fleshing out of the personality and history of the Devil and the details of the part he played. In Revelations there is a verse reading "*I saw a star fallen from heaven to earth, and he was given the key to the shaft of the bottomless pit*" (*Revelations* 9:1). In one with the earlier glossing of the passage in *Isaiah* this was now taken to refer to Satan. The implication was that on being cast out of Heaven following his defeat he was given control of Hell – another idea that was taking shape in a novel form at this time. This in turn was linked to the punishment of Adam and Eve upon their expulsion from Eden, in particular the coming of death. The orthodox narrative now became that after the Fall Satan had dominion over the Earth and that all who died, including the patriarchs and heroes of the Old Testament, would descend into Hell and be held captive by him – until that is the death and resurrection of Jesus which broke his power in that regard.

The other part of *Revelations*, and the bit that continues to fascinate an amazing number of people, was an account of the Last Days and the final war on Earth between God and the Devil and his supporters who were identified with the two Beasts of Revelation, the Beast from the Sea (666) and the Antichrist or false prophet. The usual understanding of that is that on the Second Coming of Jesus the two Beasts would be destroyed and the Devil bound for a thousand years in which Jesus would rule as an earthly monarch, after which the Devil would be released and there would be a final battle (Armageddon). The old world would then be wrapped up and the Day of Judgment would take place. This event, identified with the famous passage in *St Matthew's Gospel*, would see a general resurrection of the dead who then be judged with some going on to eternal life in the new heaven and earth created after the apocalypse while others would either be cast for eternity into the lake of burning fire, along with the Devil and those angels who had shared in his rebellion, or annihilated, experiencing a second and permanent death, according to the theology of the exegete (*Matthew* 25: 31–46).

So by about the later fourth century the essential idea and biography of the Devil had been formed, along with an idea of his part and role in the great story of the world. He was an angel, one of the greatest, who had rebelled against God through pride and had subverted many other angels to his cause (a third of them by most estimates). Following his defeat and expulsion from Heaven he had subverted the Creation by taking advantage of the free will that God had given Adam and Eve and so bringing about the Fall and the alienation of humans from God. He had been left to work his will on the world and had had custody of all who died until the ministry, death, and resurrection of Jesus who defeated him. However, he remains present and active in the world and constantly strives against God and tries to corrupt people, out of sheer spite, malice, and resentment. He is no longer the direct servant of God or a vague class of spiritual being but a definite person who is the malevolent adversary of goodness and the divine purpose. As such he is the tester who tries humanity and the world to discover their worth and who also by his activities brings about both evil but also the higher forms of good. He is an independent spiritual being and opponent of God (and so like the dark power Ahriman in Zoroastrianism) but in the Abrahamic conception he is always a subordinate power who is opposed to God but plays a part in the grand scheme of things (hard though it may be for us to grasp what it might be). The theological details were then developed by the Doctors of the Church, above all by St Augustine who combined this synthetic narrative with Platonic philosophy to create the teachings on sin and the nature of the human will that would play a central part in Christian thinking for centuries.

The story here is mainly about the development of the idea in Christianity. One way of understanding the story is to say that Christians over the early centuries of the Church put together or invented the person of Satan and his story to meet certain needs that they had, both intellectual and theological and personal (inasmuch as it helped them make sense of aspects of their own experience that would otherwise have been deeply troubling from an orthodox Christian perspective). In other words, you could say that the Devil was invented or created by the gradual process we have outlined. The alternative is the view put forward by Jeffrey Burton Russell in his magisterial multi-volume history of the Devil. In this, the process is rather one of discovery, in which Christians come to know about the Devil as they interpret both the world and texts in the light of the Gospel. Both of these ways of thinking see the Devil as coming from the need for Christians to deal with the problem of theodicy in a way that avoids either radical fatalism or the gnostic heresy that the world is created by a being who is at best incompetent at worst malign. A different more sociological or cultural explanation is given by Elaine Pagels, according to which Christians and Jews (originally) developed the idea and story of Satan as a way of demonising their opponents and making them radically 'other' and opposed to the good people or insiders. It was thus a way of defining and so strengthening an identity. This initially reflected the powerless position of Jews and Christians in the Roman Empire, but when (some) Christians gained power as a result of the conversion of Constantine it also became a way to demonise the outgroup in the subsequent internal conflicts over how to define key points of doctrine. This became a major feature of the way the idea played out in later centuries, as well shall see.

Meanwhile, the course of development in Judaism and subsequently Islam, was different in important ways. Although the idea of the Devil originated in Second Temple Judaism, following the final defeat of Jewish messianism in 153 AD the rabbis who then reconstructed the faith moved sharply away from ideas that had become widespread previously, including that of an adversary power. Instead there was a move towards (or alternatively back to) strict monotheism in which a divine power was held ultimately and directly responsible for all that happened. The apocalyptic tradition was also scaled back sharply as was the idea of an afterlife, with a movement towards the position of mortalism in which there is no afterlife (although a future resurrection is not ruled out). In Islam the idea of the Devil was found in much the same way as in Christianity (although his subordinate status was made much clearer) but details of the narrative were different. The Devil, called Iblis, was either an Angel or a djinn (a class of spiritual beings of great power but ambiguous moral status) who had defied God's order to prostrate himself before the newly created Adam, on the grounds that he, a being of fire, should not render homage to one made of mud. For this he was expelled from the divine presence and sent to earth to act as the obstructor and tempter or *shaitan*. So, his role and nature were similar to that of the Christian Devil but the associated mythology was less developed. In addition, later Islamic theologians tended to follow the same reasoning as the

Jewish rabbis and emphasised divine omnipotence to a degree that made the notion of an adversary superfluous.

In any event, regardless of what reason there may have been for the emergence of the idea, and the varying forms it took, the idea, story and image of Satan took on a life of its own. As the world moved from antiquity to the Middle Ages, the concept became far richer and more detailed and attracted to itself all kinds of other ideas and practices that came together to form a complex mythology and system of ideas, as we shall see in the next chapter.

Further Reading
All of the works cited for the Introduction and Chapter 1, plus the following.

Angier, Tom (ed.) *The History of Evil in Antiquity 2000 BCE to 450 CE*. Routledge.

Barker, Margaret (2005) *The Lost Prophet: The Book of Enoch and its Influence on Christianity*. Sheffield Phoenix Press.

Charlesworth, James H. (2007) *The Old Testament Pseudepigrapha Vol. 1: Apocalyptic Literature and Testaments*. Yale University Press.

Forsyth, Neill (1987) *The Old Enemy: Satan and the Combat Myth*. Princeton University Press

Graves, Kersey (1924) *The Biography of Satan*. Peter Eckler.

Kelly, Henry Ansgar (2006) *Satan: A Biography*. Cambridge University Press.

Orlov, Andrei A. (2011) *Dark Mirrors: Azazel and Satanael in Early Jewish Demonology*. State University of New York Press

Pagels, Elaine (1996) *The Origin of Satan*. Vintage.

Russell, Jeffrey Burton (1977) *The Devil: Perceptions of Evil from Antiquity to Primitive Christianity*. Cornell University Press.

Russell, Jeffrey Burton 1981. *Satan: The Early Christian Tradition*. Cornell University Press.

Chapter 3. The Devil in the Middle Ages

As the ancient world passed away and was replaced by the Christian and Islamic world of the Middle Ages, so the figure of the Devil, formed in the latter part of the previous era, became more detailed. In a time when large parts of the world were dominated by two monotheistic faiths in which he played a prominent part, he came to bulk larger in the thought and narratives of the time. Indeed, a key feature of the mental life of almost everyone at this time, whether educated or not and whatever their social status, was that the Devil and his workings were a central and normal part of their way of thinking about the world.

He was simply assumed and taken for granted in understanding or explaining events in a way that is now foreign to us. During this period the narrative and persona that had been worked out by the time of the late Roman Empire was fleshed out and given detail. Partly this involved a working out and elaboration of the theology around him and much greater detail about exactly how he worked to realise his purposes. It also involved the incorporation into Christian thinking of details and narratives from the older pagan religions, often transmogrified or reversed (a phenomenon not confined to thinking about Satan, as the many cases of saints who were thinly disguised versions of gods and goddesses attests). The medieval period also saw the production of all sorts of curious myths, often with a tenuous Biblical foundation, and some of these had the Devil as a prominent figure or playing an active background role, while he also appeared frequently in both popular and elite culture. Towards the end of the period a new set of ideas began to appear and spread, not inevitably associated with the Devil but which came to be attached to him because of the way the Church thought about these matters and this pointed the way towards a much more profound transformation of the idea of the Devil that took place during the subsequent period of the Renaissance and Reformation and subsequently, which we look at in the next chapter.

The theology of Satan was worked out in the Christian world mainly by St Augustine, and his approach remained the predominant one for centuries until it was amended in the later part of the Medieval period (although the initial criticisms were made in the twelfth century). The central point was the one set out briefly earlier, that the Devil was the active agent in both his own fall and that of Adam and Eve. Created sinless, and with a perfect will like all angels (so that he can never regret or repent his rebellion) he brought about the fall of man and so condemned all future generations to death and to be in his power. This meant that the original creation was perfectly good and remains essentially good, though marred by the consequences of Satan's rebellion. (This argument was made in opposition to the gnostic view that the physical world was evil, a domain of suffering created by a malevolent power). Evil for Augustine was the radical weakening or absence of the good, a spoiling or perversion of what was originally good rather than a positive thing in its own right and this defined the Devil's essentially negative quality and character. This in turn defined the central concept of Christianity, that of salvation, and hence of the meaning of the life, death, and resurrection of Jesus. For Augustine what Jesus did by his freely accepted death on the cross was to redeem humanity from the Devil's power. He gave his own life to Satan in exchange for the lives of all those who otherwise were in the Devil's grip, from all times. This is sometimes known as the 'ransom' theory of salvation. The point of course was that because Jesus was, as the Son, the second person the Trinity and so God as well as man, the Devil was unable to keep him in his power and so the 'deal' was one sided.

This theology was severely criticised by later Christian thinkers and replaced eventually by the idea of atonement (originally put forward by the eleventh century theologian and Archbishop of Canterbury, Saint Anselm, in his *Cur Deus Homo*) in which Jesus's freely chosen death makes up for the original fall of Adam and Eve. However, it was Augustine's view that remained the dominant one throughout the Middle Ages and shaped the development of both popular and elite thinking at the time where the Devil was concerned. This took a number of forms. Once was the development of narratives based on Christian teaching but which were not clearly Biblical in their origins, a set of additions to the Christian story of the Devil. One of the most important was that of the Harrowing of Hell. This derived from Augustine's theology and one line from the Apostles Creed which says of Jesus *"He died, and was buried. He descended into Hell"*. When Jesus died, like all men before him, he descended into Hell as a result of the original Fall. Once in Hell, he engaged in combat with the Devil and defeated and bound him. Hell could not contain him and Death had no power over him because he was God as well as Man. During the time he spent in Hell he also preached the Gospel to the dead who were there and freed the patriarchs and heroes of the Old Testament. He then returned from Hell in the Resurrection, leaving the defeated Satan behind him and bursting open the gates of Hell. The Harrowing of Hell, often thought of as a one to one combat both spiritual and physical, was frequently portrayed in art and became another central event in the story.

The other thing that was worked out in much greater detail was that of Hell, which was made a real and intensely imagined place in Medieval thought. This is dealt with in Chapter 6 so we need not go into it here. One part of Christian teaching that did receive great elaboration at this time and was connected to the concepts of both Hell and the Devil, was that of the Last Judgment. This is a long-standing part of Christian teaching, derived from one of the most powerful and arresting passages of the New Testament, in the twenty fifth chapter of St Matthew's Gospel. Here Jesus tells his disciples that at some point in the future he will return, not as he was when he spoke to them (a carpenter) but as a King, in his full power and glory. He will then summon all of the people of the world (believed because of texts elsewhere to include everyone who had ever lived) before him and divide them *"as a shepherd divides the sheep from the goats, with the sheep on the right and the goats on the left"*. The sheep are praised for performing the Acts of Mercy (feeding the hungry, giving drink to the thirsty, taking in strangers, clothing the naked, and visiting the sick and imprisoned) and are welcomed into everlasting life in Heaven. The goats are cursed for failing to do these things and are cast into the lake of fire "prepared for the Devil and His angels" and condemned to everlasting punishment.

This passage was interpreted (among many other things) to say something about the place of the Devil in the overall story and his role between the Harrowing and the final judgment. Life it was thought, was a kind of test or trial, of one's virtue and ability to resist temptation. The Devil was a kind of examiner or tester, whose function was to lead people astray and away from the paths of virtue (like the goats). He would know that this was in some sense futile, as he was defeated and condemned, but in his rage and despair he sought anyway to corrupt the innocent and to deface virtue, this being an end in itself despite his defeat. The concept of life as a trial with the Devil as a seducer and everything leading to a final verdict and judgment was one that made sense because of his core quality of pure malevolence and this was used to explain how he passed his time while awaiting the Second Coming.

Another set of Christian narratives where the Devil often made an appearance was that of lives of saints, which were turned out in large numbers during the medieval period. In these he often presents challenges or tests for the Saint, seeking to divert them from their path and to mislead or obstruct them. These accounts usually have physical descriptions of Satan and his actions. One in particular was to have a long-lasting impact as far as the way the Devil and his activities were understood and portrayed. This was the life of the Egyptian monk and founder of monasticism, St Anthony. Living in the third and fourth centuries and spending much of his life as a hermit in the Eastern Desert, his life was written up by his contemporary Athanasius of Alexandria. The *Life of Saint Anthony* contains descriptions of his being tempted and attacked by the Devil and other demons, all of them trying to turn him from the path of virtue. They appear to him in a series of forms and shapes, some bizarre and grotesque, others beautiful (notably the form of a beautiful woman). In late Antiquity these visions or experiences were only part of the longer story but in the Middle Ages they came to be the main focus for readers, because of the way they spoke to the growing interest in the way Satan interacted with individual human beings at the level of human consciousness and perception. The temptation of Saint Anthony became the subject of art and storytelling (much of it with a surreal quality) and it became the main source for subsequent stories and images of the Devil's interaction with the human world.

Alongside the expanded body of Christian narratives were essentially pagan myths that were incorporated into the Medieval Christian world view, not least where the Devil was concerned. The most prominent of these was the physical identification of Satan with the Greek god of nature, Pan. It is during the Middle Ages that the Devil comes to be envisioned as having the physical appearance of Pan, human from the waist up but with goat's legs, ears, and horns. Dragon myths, which had been a prominent feature of the ancient world, were also incorporated into Christian stories, with dragons seen as dark and demonic creatures or as the actual embodiment of the Devil himself (it is this that leads to the persistent trope in Western dragon myths of their being subtle, devious, and psychologically subversive). This idea actually originates in the pagan religions of ancient Mesopotamia, where the dragon is the form taken by the forces of chaos and disorder such as the goddess Tiamat, defeated by Marduk. The narrative passed into parts of the Old Testament Apocrypha, notably the legend of Bel and the Dragon (sometimes included in the *Book of Daniel*). From there it became part of Christian belief. The dragon is also a feature of the mythology of the Germanic peoples and so these myths were also incorporated into popular Christian narratives. For the Church the deities of the pagan religions and the plethora of nature spirits, supernatural beings, and spirits of place that had so filled up the mental worlds of pagan Europeans, were all declared to be agents of the Devil, demonic powers and fallen angels like himself (see Chapter 7). This made Satan and his servants something almost omnipresent, found in every part and aspect of the world, and gave him a whole range of specific local associations.

A major part of the consolidation of the idea of the Devil during the Middle Ages was the creation of a definite idea of his physical appearance, something that had not happened in the early Church. This has proved to be very persistent so the image that medieval artists and storytellers created is one that is still familiar and recognisable, as well as still being used by artists and illustrators. This persistent image existed despite one of his features in the medieval imagination being that he is a shape-shifter, able to take on almost any form he likes. The idea was that despite his appearing in any number of guises (as he did to the unfortunate Saint Anthony) he has an underlying true appearance, and can be forced to resume that shape and also often adopts it anyway. The predominant medieval vision of the devil has him as bestial and grotesque, often combining features of the human with the animal. As well as the association with the goat he is also often shown with bat like wings, this being an inverse of the usual depiction of angels as winged, with the wings changed from the light plumage of the angel to the leathery ones of demons. (This of course refers to his origins as a fallen angel). Sometimes he has six wings – this comes from the identification of Lucifer, the rebel angel, with the six-winged seraphs described in a vision in the *Book of Ezekiel*, the seraphs being the highest order of angels and those closest to God. He is usually described as hairy (the hair is often red) and when he speaks his voice is hoarse and cracked. These last two reflect one of the limitations of his shape-shifting ability: he can never adopt a perfect form but is always flawed or deformed in some way. This is an outward reflection of his inner corruption. In addition to a detailed set of physical qualities, he came to have a whole series of associations, with particular animals (the snake, the ass, the ape), with salt water and the ocean (as opposed to fresh water and the littoral seas), with certain times of the year and days, with colours (most obviously black but also red and yellow), even with certain musical intervals (see below Chapter 11).

One definite feature of the medieval version of Satan is his intense physicality. Although ultimately a spiritual being, he was thought of and portrayed as physical and concrete. This can be seen in the descriptions of his appearance, which dwell on specific physical details. There were a number of reasons for this emphasis. One was that it reflected his fallen state. In being cast out of Heaven and falling to earth he became part of the material world and took on material shape and qualities. The physical is also lower than the spiritual in the hierarchical understanding of the universe that was central to medieval thought and so in some ways the Devil, as the lowest of creatures was also the most physical. This also went along with a stress on the physical reality of Hell and its torments, which was an important part of Church teaching at the time (See Chapter 6 below). The Devil's physical presence and nature also explains his constant appearance in the real world, his regularly being perceived by the senses and his playing an active role in actual events, even if only through agents.

Alongside his material nature was another quality that is almost universal in the medieval accounts. Although the Devil is still powerful and able to do great harm to people, he is also utterly defeated. He was totally defeated by Jesus during the Harrowing of Hell and by the redemptive sacrifice of the crucifixion and so he is bound, unable claim human lives and souls in the way he could before. This state of total defeat was best captured in the work that summed up the medieval vision of both the Devil and Hell, the *Divine Comedy* of Dante. At the end of the first part of that great work Dante sees Satan at the very bottom of hell. He is a huge, hairy, monstrous figure, with six bat-like wings and three faces on his head – a blasphemous version of the Trinity perhaps. He is eternally bound, frozen to his chest in the icy lake of Cocytus. His wings beat frantically but serve only to send a wind through Hell that freezes the lake and so he remains forever imprisoned. All he can do is to endlessly flay and chew on the three arch sinners who are imprisoned in his three mouths (Brutus, Cassius, and Judas Iscariot) while he weeps tears of rage and despair that run down his faces and mingle with the bloody slaver that drips from his mouths. A more arresting picture of helpless frustration and defeat is hard to imagine.

Despite his abject and defeated state, the Devil in these accounts is still fearsome and terrifying, in the way that a caged and venomous beast is. He still has the power to damn and destroy people and will do so until he is finally cast into the lake of fire at the end of time. However, just as people can only be harmed by a caged beast, however venomous, if they put themselves in its reach, so men and women can put themselves in the Devil's power by succumbing to his blandishments, even though he is defeated. The way this happened was one of the great additions made to the idea of the Devil by medieval thinkers and it related to the working out of the mechanism of his main activity, the tempting and misleading of people. This was done initially by Pope Gregory the Great, in a process of working out the implications of Augustine's ideas about sin and the frailty of the human will. One of the things Augustine had worked out was the way the fallen nature of humanity showed itself in the will, the active and deciding part of the human mind. The essential result of the Fall was that the human will was corrupted and no longer perfect. As such people were led to desire and do things that ultimately, they did not want to do. As the key text from Saint Paul put it *"the evil that I would not do I do; the good that I would do I do not"*. (Romans 7: 18–20).

The question was how had the Devil initially corrupted the will of Adam and Eve? What Gregory did was to work out in more detail not only how this was done but also how Satan continued to do this with their descendants. He described a three part process: initially the Devil planted suggestions or ideas into the mind of his subject, which were carefully designed to appeal to the particular mental qualities of that person; then the ideas lead to speculation and provoke a pleasant experience or sensation in the mind of the subject; finally the person acts on and realises the original suggestion to some extent, maybe completely. This subtle and powerful description of mental processes did two things.

It explained and made sense of a common human experience and it explained how the Devil was still able to work away in the world even in his defeated condition. There were protections against him, above all that of the Church through the sacraments of baptism and communion but outside those protections all were at the mercy of his unseen yet effective subversion.

At the same time the Devil appeared in popular legends and fictions, and in these he is very much active still in the physical world. All over Europe there are monuments or natural features that are associated with him, usually with a story involving him to explain their existence. He also appears in the popular fiction of the period such as Miracle plays, staged enactments of Biblical stories that look more like pantomime to the modern eye. In these kinds of tales, he is dangerous and unfriendly but also grotesque and even comical – a frequent theme is his being tricked by a quick-witted interlocutor, very often a saint. The humour however has a different quality to its modern counterpart, because this is a matter of making jokes about something that underneath the levity is taken very seriously. The key point is that the Devil and his actions are seen as a well-known part of the natural order, something that explains many phenomena in an unforced and natural way. This is true for both the writings of the learned and also popular tales – the authors of both lived in a world where Satan was a leading figure. It is notable though that in elite literature the Devil appears mainly in works of scholarship such as theology and homily. He does not appear very often in elite literature from this period and in particular is not a character in chivalric romances and legends. It is popular literature both entertaining and moralistic where he plays a central part. As the Middle Ages progressed his active role became even more worked out and it came to be combined with another intellectual inheritance from the ancient world and this combination was to prove hugely important for both the intellectual and social history of Europe, once it reached its full development during the Renaissance. This was the notion of ritual magic or sorcery.

Ritual magic as an idea and practice appears in one form or another in almost every human civilisation and culture that we know of. The fundamental idea of ritual magic is that by certain exercises or procedures or disciplined effort of the mind and will, it is possible to bring about or avert events or transformations in the physical world and the mental world of humans. This is a way of thinking and a set of practices associated with it that is distinct from both religion and science, although there are similarities and overlaps between all three of these modes of thought and understanding of the world. Magic, like religion, typically becomes systematic and organised with time, developing into elaborate structures of thought. We can thus identify and trace magical thinking and its patterns in all of the world's civilisations. Typically it takes two forms: there is popular magic, practised and used by the common people and concerned with the kinds of matters that bulk large in their lives such as love, money and good fortune, health, and enmity (the latter taking the form of charms or procedures to either bring harm to somebody or defend against such an assault). There is also the more elevated and systematic magic of the elite, more abstract and theoretical (and hence often connected to what we think of as science and scientific disciplines), more systematic and worked out, and concerned with things such as power, knowledge, and control of the world and one's own fate, as well as the more mundane matters.

This was as true of the classical civilisation of the Roman Empire as of any other. Several forms of ritual magic were widely practised there, most notably divination and the creation of charms or amulets, but including others as well. Much of the magical traditions of classical Rome came from territories that the Romans had conquered. The most important was Egypt, renowned from an early date as a place of great occult (or hidden) knowledge. During the history of the Empire and even before it, this tradition of magic spread throughout the lands around the Mediterranean and beyond. It was thus an important part of the life of the world within which Christianity took shape. The response of the Church Fathers and subsequently the institutional Church was apparently clear but actually ambivalent. The initial response, which was also the orthodox one throughout the history of the Church, was to condemn all forms of magic, from divination to spells, charms, and amulets as impious and blasphemous (even more so the darker and higher forms of magic such as speaking to or even raising the dead). The essential argument was firstly that such practices were presumptuous because they presumed or claimed powers and knowledge that were only appropriate to God or his agents, and secondly that they were also cheats and frauds. It was a short step from this view to associating all such practices with the machinations of the Evil One. Islamic theologians have also taken this view, and continue to do so. The practice of magic, particularly in its more elaborate and ritual forms was therefore condemned by the early Church and this view was reiterated with force by the medieval Church. In this context the key figure was the Biblical one of Simon Magus, who appears as a figure in the Acts of the Apostles, in which he engages in a metaphysical duel with Saint Peter (*Acts* 8: 9–24.) A great deal of apocryphal legend came to cluster around the figure of Simon and he came to be the archetypal magician or sorcerer in later Christian thinking. He was supposed for example to have been able to levitate and fly without support. This showed the tension within the Church's view because the practice of magic was held to be fraudulent yet the powers derived from it could be real and effectual.

Moreover, there was also another side to the Medieval Church's view of magic. The stories of the doings of the Saints and Apostles, the old testament prophets such as Elijah, and even those of the acts and miracles of Jesus himself are full of events that fit the traditional idea of magic. There was a strong element of magic in other words to the traditions of the Christian faith itself. From that point of view, it was not so much the powers or the practice that mattered but the source of the power and the ends to which it was used. As Christianity spread throughout Europe during the early Middle Ages so we can see both tendencies at work. On the one hand the Church destroyed both the older pagan religions and the magical beliefs and practices associated with them, demolishing sacred sites and uprooting groves and punishing observance of both religious rituals and customary magical practices. On the other, many pagan sites or sanctuaries were transformed into churches and much traditional practice, particularly customary magic, was incorporated into Church rituals and practices and so Christianised. This meant that the idea of magic was not totally rooted out but survived within the everyday practice of the Church. In addition, certain elite traditions survived in a purer form. The most important of these was hermeticism.

Hermeticism was a mystery tradition that can be traced back as far as the second century BC, named after the mythical figure of Hermes Trismegistus (Thrice-Greatest Hermes). It was associated with other developments in late paganism such as Neo-Platonism. An important aspect of hermeticism was the use of ritual magic to summon spiritual beings and control them and to manipulate and direct natural forces. As such it was an example of the higher form of magic as well as being a type of mysticism and mystery religion.

Hermetic texts survived the collapse of classical civilisation and began to circulate in Europe in the later part of the medieval period. One of the central ideas that came out of this was that of the adept or magus. This was a person who had mastered themselves and their own nature and also a number of arts and so acquired great power and knowledge. In Hermeticism the Magus had an almost demi-god like status and powers and the idea grew that this was a goal that people could pursue through systematic study. This idea began to feature in elite thinking from the fourteenth century onwards, as the Middle Ages waned and a new era began, that of the Renaissance. Part of Hermeticism and ritual magic was the idea of summoning and controlling spirits and in particular fallen angels or demons. By the later Middle Ages therefore we get the start of the idea of Black Magic, of ritual magic that was not only dark in the sense of being used for harmful or morally dubious ends (this idea is found in the magical systems of all societies and civilisations) but also dark because it involved intimate congress and communication with the Prince of Darkness himself.

The Middle Ages saw the Devil, as he had been worked out or discovered by late antiquity, incorporated into both the intellectual world of the elite and the rich and diverse one of popular culture. In both cases there were additions made to his story and to the understanding of his nature. Some of these additions came from exploring the implications of the theology and the narrative founded upon a certain kind of biblical exegesis that had been formulated by the early fifth century. Others came from elements of non-Christian belief that were incorporated into the world-view of Medieval Christian Europe or were generated spontaneously by the ferment of popular culture. By the end of the high Middle Ages his identity and the image of him that existed in the minds of Europeans had acquired firm and definite contours and features. The main ones in addition to the core features set out earlier were that he was an actual physical being, intensely and grotesquely so in fact, who nonetheless was active in the minds and souls of men and women and still walking up and down the world. Despite this he was ultimately defeated and bound and only active because he was allowed liberty to do his work by the victorious divine power that had terminated his rule of the world and people's souls with the Crucifixion and Resurrection. This work was to tempt and test humanity, to try them as it was said. He would continue doing this until the end of days (thought to be at an indeterminate date in the future but not that remote) when he would be allowed one last great rebellion before being bound for even and his remaining role ended. All this was a settled belief for several centuries. As the Middle Ages waned and society changed however, so this view came to change. The essential core idea remained constant, but during the period we now call the Renaissance the rest underwent radical change. Satan underwent a regeneration we might say and he emerged as far more powerful than before.

Further Reading

Butler, Elizabeth M. (1993, 1st published 1948) *The Myth of the Magus*. Cambridge University Press.

Collins, David J. (ed.) (2019) *The Sacred and the Sinister: Studies in Medieval Religion and Magic*. Pennsylvania State University Press.

Collins, David J. (ed.) (2018) *The Cambridge History of Magic and Witchcraft in the West From Antiquity to the Present*. Cambridge University Press.

Fanger, Claire (ed.) (1998) *Conjuring Spirits: Texts and Traditions of Medieval Ritual Magic*. Sutton.

Forsyth, Neill (2003) *The Satanic Epic*. Princeton University Press.

Jolly, Karen (2001) "Medieval Magic: Definitions, Beliefs, Practices" in Bengt Ankarloo & Stuart Clark (eds) *Witchcraft and Magic in Europe: The Middle Ages*. 1–72. University of Pennsylvania Press.

Kieckheffer, Richard (1997) *Forbidden Rites: A Necromancer's Manual of the Fifteenth Century*. Sutton.

Maxwell-Stuart, P. G. (2005) *The Occult in Mediaeval Europe, 500–1500*. Palgrave.

Peters, Edward (2001) "The Medieval Church and State on Superstition, Magic, and Witchcraft: From Augustine to the Sixteenth Century" in Bengt Ankarloo & Stuart Clark (eds) *Witchcraft and Magic in Europe: The Middle Ages* 173–245. Pennsylvania University Press.

Pinsent, Andrew (ed.) (2018) *The History of Evil in the Middle Ages 450–1450 CE*. Routledge.

Russell, Jeffry Burton (1984) *Lucifer: The Devil in the Middle Ages.* Cornell University Press.

Trachtenberg, Joshua (1995 1st published 1943) *The Devil and the Jews: The Medieval Conception of the Jew and Its Relation to Modern Anti-Semitism.* Jewish Publications Society.

Bailey, Michael D. (2003) *Battling Demons: Witchcraft, Heresy, and Reform in the Late Middle Ages.* Pennsylvania State University Press.

Chapter 4: The Renaissance and the Transformation of The Devil

As the fourteenth century passed and was succeeded by the fifteenth it became clear even to people at the time that there was a profound change taking place in the cultural and intellectual life of Europe.

Historians have come to retrospectively speak of the Renaissance, using the term first employed by the nineteenth century Swiss historian Jacob Burckhardt in his book *The Civilisation of the Renaissance in Italy*. The term Renaissance referred to what he saw as the central feature of the intellectual life of the time, the rebirth or rediscovery of the learning and ideas of the classical world. The term remains in use because it captured something, the process of intellectual and artistic ferment and exploration of new ideas that we can see all over Europe. The period is usually defined as covering the fifteenth and sixteenth centuries but many historians push the origins of the period back into the second half of the fourteenth century. The intellectual process we can observe during the Renaissance was not a break with the ideas and intellectual life of the Middle Ages but a process of exploration in which concepts and ideas were pushed in new directions and in the process changed and extended but without the core idea being abandoned. There was thus an element of continuity and extension as well as novelty. The genuinely new elements tended to come from the rediscovery of classical texts and learning (in many cases this was a matter not so much of actual rediscovery as of a change in emphasis and interests, with texts that had previously been overlooked being studied). There was also great interest in ideas and insights gained from contact with the Islamic world.

The historical context for this era of intellectual exploration was actually grim. The central decades of the fourteenth century saw the arrival in Europe of the Black Death, which in just a few years carried off between a third and just under a half of the continent's population. Simultaneously, the Earth's climate took a turn for the worse as far as human beings were concerned, with the advent of the 'Little Ice Age'. The fall in temperatures led to more frequent wet Summers and harsh Winters and so made harvest failures and famines more common. The plague meanwhile recurred at regular intervals and there were also more frequent outbreaks of other diseases such as typhus than had been the case earlier. After Columbus returned from the New World his crewmen brought back another scourge in the form of syphilis which rapidly spread all over Europe. In addition, this was an age of war, increasingly deadly in its impact because of developments in military technology, above all gunpowder.

The Renaissance was also the age of the Military Revolution, with armies becoming much larger than those of the Medieval period and also permanent (unlike the short-lived forces of the Middle Ages, which were typically only raised for a campaign season and then reassembled). Because of the advent of artillery and firearms and the development of new methods of fighting war became much more devastating. There was also an increase in atrocities as a feature of warfare, enormously aggravated by the religious divisions in Europe from the 1520s onwards. In the fifteenth and sixteenth centuries warfare was incessant – there was always a war going on somewhere in Europe. This brought devastation and suffering to civilians as armies laid lands waste and brought famine and disease in their wake. It was actually the parts of Europe most associated with the culture of the Renaissance (Italy and the Low Countries) that bore the brunt of this.

The two and a half centuries of the Renaissance were thus an age of intellectual and cultural exploration and discovery but also of death and suffering. The latter is captured in much of the art of the time, such as Breughel's *The Triumph of Death* which shows a ravaged and hell-like landscape with humans tormented by fire and monstrous creatures (symbolising plague and natural disasters but also literal as well as figurative demons). The omnipresence of death and destruction as well as novelty and creation shaped much of the intellectual changes. Above all, it brought about a transformation in the dominant idea and image of the Devil. This process fitted exactly the model described – the core ideas that had been fleshed out in Late Antiquity and the Middle Ages continued but they came to be understood in a clearly different way, with a markedly different set of emphases. The predominant understanding of his nature changed, he became seen as more active and also more powerful than had been thought in the Middle Ages, and therefore more threatening, his personality and appearance altered. Alongside this and feeding into it, were changes in the way Hell and demons were understood and a massive expansion of the ideas of ritual magic that had started to appear in the later Middle Ages.

The recurrent natural disasters and constant wars of the Renaissance made the question of divine justice (theodicy) seem more pressing to many thoughtful people. How and why was such suffering and wickedness allowed by an all-powerful and beneficent God? One answer was that this was punishment for sin and wickedness on the part of human beings, particularly the wealthy and powerful and those who should know better, above all the clergy. This led initially to movements for religious reform among the laity, such as the Brethren of the Common Life, founded in the later fifteenth century and associated with figures such as Erasmus and Thomas A Kempis. These involved living a personal life of piety and abstemiousness while also engaging in study and contemplation. There had been movements for reform like this before in the history of the Church but this time they were not contained within the bounds of the Church and its theology and the result was the Reformation, which destroyed the unity of Christendom and made the wars and conflicts of the times much more bitter and savage. On both sides of this divide we can see two tendencies, arising from both the new learning and in response to the circumstances of the time, and it was these that transformed the understanding of the Devil.

The first was the awareness of evil in human affairs as well as nature. The obvious answer for all Christians as to where these came from was that they were the work of the Devil, directly or indirectly. The conclusion that both Protestants and Catholics came to was that he was more active than they had supposed and his handiwork came to be seen everywhere. This was the first big change. In the Middle Ages Satan was active but ultimately defeated, however much people might fear him. In the Renaissance he became much more active, at work in the natural world, in politics and public affairs, and in private life. One aspect of this was the sudden emergence of the belief that he had an army of human servants who had entered into pacts or agreements with him – a notion that had catastrophic results when it interacted with the legal system as we see in more detail in Chapter 8. This meant again that he became far more threatening, the head of a vast and malevolent conspiracy working everywhere to do ill and oppose the good. The Devil of the Renaissance was not only more active but far more powerful

– to the point where some Protestant thinkers in particular came close to the heresy of Dualism and making him an independent power in his own right. The emphasis on his power and ability to do things in the human world explained straightforwardly why there was so much sin, evil, and suffering in the world. Just as the actual world of Europeans was one of constant warfare, so this was projected onto the spiritual world, which came to be seen as a site of constant combat and struggle, with the Devil the commander-in-chief of one of the two sides. He came to loom much larger and have a more prominent place in the way the world was pictured than he had in the Middle Ages.

One of the sites of combat in this spiritual warfare was the minds of individual men and women. This meant that all good Christians had to be constantly on guard against the temptations and suggestions of the Evil One. One of the features of the revival of piety that was so prominent in the Renaissance and Reformation was an emphasis on introspection and self-examination, a process of permanent self-questioning. This found expression in a new genre of writing, that of the confessional autobiography, with examples produced by figures among both Catholic and Protestant. (Both looked back to the example of St Augustine, whose *Confessions* was the model for this kind of account). Frequently this introspection led to a heightened awareness of the darker side of one's own nature and this became a constant awareness of the incessant efforts of Satan to pervert the course of both thought and action. This again emphasised just how active and powerful he was but it also gave him other novel qualities.

One was that the Devil became far more subtle and guileful as his role as a tempter was emphasised. The straightforward and physical temptations that were a feature of Saints lives and Medieval morality plays were supplemented by an array of more indirect psychological temptations and lures and so the Devil came to be thought of as inventive, supple, devious, and sophisticated. He became far more attractive and even fascinating. He also became far more spiritual or psychological as an entity. As we have seen, the Devil of the Middle Ages as found in Dante was grossly physical. The Devil of the Renaissance was reinvented as a spiritual power. He might take physical form but that was a secondary feature: the primary reality was that he existed in the mental and spiritual world. This meant he could be found anywhere and could not be contained. An important aspect of this was that he became identified with the element of air, meaning that he could travel like the wind anywhere in the sublunary sphere of the earth and its surroundings (everything above the Moon was Heaven and so barred to him).This was a major change to the way he was understood. It made him less grotesque and physically threatening but, in many ways, darker and more intimidating. It also meant that Hell became less a physical place than a state of mind and the work of Satan became not so much a matter of physical intervention in the world as of being a dark and pervasive influence in the mental life of people.

One feature of the Devil's nature that had been there from the start was that he was a lord, the Prince of Darkness. He had been among the greatest of angels and was still first among those who had fallen. In addition, he was still allowed great power after his fall, even after his defeat in the Harrowing of Hell. What changed was the image of his Lordship, the way it was imagined. This again was in some ways a reflection of changes that were taking place in reality. The Renaissance saw the decline of the superior powers of the Empire and the Papacy and a corresponding increase in the power and autonomy of kings and princes and other rulers. The innovations in warfare also increased the power of monarchs (who could afford the new weapons) and reduced that of the aristocracy (who usually could not). This rise of 'new monarchies' was projected onto the Devil. He became a Renaissance prince or ruler and acquired the appearance and qualities of real-life figures such as the Italian rulers that Machiavelli described from life in *The Prince*. His physical appearance and dress were less often the bestial guise he had during the Middle Ages. Instead he became elegant, well-dressed, and handsome. He became charming, and refined, but also a master of treachery, betrayal, and ruthless cruelty. The similarity between this image and the description (and advice) that Machiavelli gave was noted by contemporaries – hence Old Nick (from Niccolo) becoming one of his names. His court and kingdom also became like a Renaissance monarch's, with elaborate degrees and hierarchies and the many subordinate demon-lords became a dark image of the aristocracy of the Renaissance court and Church.

This meant that instead of being the brutish creature of the Middle Ages, the Devil (and his fellow fallen angels) became more refined and aristocratic. He became above all, more intellectual. He was now learned, a master of elaborate argument and immensely knowledgeable. This knowledge could bring great power and benefit but it always came with a price and was used, given his nature, to bring about the destruction and damnation of as many people as possible. This was the start of the association of the Devil with systematic knowledge and even science, something that was further developed later, in the modern world. In the Renaissance the idea of the Devil as knowledgeable, and through that a source of power, became embodied in one of the great myths of modern times. This was the myth of Faust. There was a real-life person by that name, who lived in Germany between roughly 1480 and 1540, but almost nothing is known about him for certain. What is certain was that by the 1580s he had become the subject of a mythical narrative which has since inspired a whole series of famous works, such as Goethe's *Faust*, the *Tragical History of Doctor Faustus* by Christopher Marlowe, and *The Master and Margarita* by Mikhail Bulgakov. It has also inspired many works of music and film. The details vary from one account to another but the underlying story is this: Faust is a learned scholar who is dissatisfied with human knowledge and longs for greater knowledge and power. To obtain this he enters into a pact or contract with the Devil, in the shape of his emissary Mephistopheles, who he has evoked and called up via a ceremony of ritual magic. Mephistopheles gives him great power and the ability to realise his secret desires and wishes and the knowledge of all things including things unknown to everyone else. This is time limited and after a given number of years Faust must pay by surrendering his soul to the devil who will take him to hell. In some versions, such as Goethe's he is saved at the end through the intercession of his servant Gretchen but in most, he pays the price of his contract and is damned.

This is a myth of immense power, which clearly speaks to something profound in the modern mind. Just as the historical King Arthur has faded and been replaced by an elaborate and adaptable myth so the historical doctor of theology has been supplanted by a mythical figure. The myth's power and fascination come from the way it speaks to the ambivalence of the modern world about scientific knowledge and the technological prowess it has brought. This is beneficial and makes life easier, as the knowledge gained by Faustus does for him, but there is the uneasy feeling that it comes with a price, not immediately apparent but sure to be paid in the end. The important thing is that the Devil (as Mephistopheles) is central to the story and it does not work without him. The idea of the transcending of limits and the achievement of unlimited power, knowledge, wealth, and pleasure is intimately associated from the

Renaissance onwards with the idea of a malevolent power who offers these benefits as part of a trap, a temptation to lead people astray. This is because the aspiration to such power is impious and sinful. It involves human beings attempting to acquire the powers and attributes that are appropriate only to God or at most angels (such as living forever for example). As in Paradise, what the Devil offers is forbidden knowledge.

One feature of the Faust accounts that would become very important in the modern world's image of the Devil is that Mephistopheles is playful and humorous. This was another feature that the Devil acquired during the Renaissance, he became witty, playful, amusing, yet also cynical and cruel. The main feature of his myth that comes to consciousness in the story of Faust is another aspect of his greater power and agency at this time. This is the idea that not only does he have immense knowledge and consequently powers and capacities, he can give or transmit these to people. This is always done through a formal process that involves a contract or pact and the employment of ritual magic. These ideas had been found in the Middle Ages but were not so prominent. They suddenly moved to the centre stage in the second half of the fifteenth century, as ritual magic became a much more significant part of the intellectual world of Europeans. This was one area where the crucial thing was the rediscovery of ancient thought, above all of Hermeticism.

As explained in the previous chapter, one of the things we can see in the second half of the Middle Ages is a growth of interest in formalised, ritual magic (as opposed to the less systematic folk magic traditions). A key part of this was the rediscovery of the intellectual tradition of Hermeticism, as it had been written down in the second century AD, mainly in Egypt. Some writings were known throughout the Medieval period but the key event was the rediscovery of the central text, the *Corpus Hermeticus*, in around 1460 and its translation in 1463 by the humanist scholar Marsilio Ficino. As the fifteenth century progressed Hermeticism (or Western Esotericism as it is now sometimes called) became one of the major intellectual interests of the Renaissance scholars and humanists. Hermeticism is a very complex and elaborate body of thought but it has easily identifiable core ideas. The foundational one is that there is a single true theology that is found in all religions but which is concealed in most of them by outward forms with the foundational truth known only to initiates of people who have made intensive study. (This is still a popular notion today under the name of the 'perennial philosophy'). It is thus a variety of mystery religion but with the feature of claiming that all religions are founded on the truth (so a follower of any religion can also study Hermeticism).

The second core idea is usually summarised as 'As above, so below'. This means that the entire universe is organised in a hierarchy, with the same type of structure and organisation repeated at each level. It also means that something that happens at one level also happens at the other levels. This was expressed by Renaissance thinkers in the idea of microcosm (the individual human being) and macrocosm (the larger universe) with each a replica of the other. This meant that events in the larger cosmos would have an impact at the level of the individual and also the opposite. It also means that by understanding the one you get greater understanding of the other. This provides a theoretical basis for magic as it means that creating an effect in oneself can produce a corresponding effect in the material world. It also meant that study of the external world could bring greater self-understanding while introspection and meditation would bring greater mastery of the outside world. This study of both the self and the external world had three aspects. Two of them, alchemy (meaning much more than transmuting base metal into gold), and astrology need not detain us here. It is the third that concerns us – theurgy.

Theurgy is the ritual aspect of hermeticism. It refers to the use of ritual to evoke and control spiritual powers and (on the principle of 'as above so below) using them to bring about physical results in the here and now. The spirits evoked and employed are benign, angelic beings. This linked to the notion of a project or study that could lead to the person undertaking it become a figure with near divine powers – a Magus. What this led to in the hands of Renaissance scholars was an elaborate and systematic magical theory and practice. The practical goals of this were knowledge and power. The power brought control over oneself, the natural world and, it was hoped, the realm of chance and fortune. There were a number of authors who developed this complex body of interconnected ideas, sometimes in the form of major and systematic treatises. To the modern mind these show a curious combination of science and superstition but in fact they were the product of a separate system of thought, close to modern science but different. One of the most systematic and extensive was the *Four Books of Natural Philosophy*, by the seventeenth century German scholar, Henry

Cornelius Agrippa. What though did these ideas have to with the Devil? As well as theurgy, there was also goetia, its dark side. This involved summoning up dark powers, demons and fallen spirits, and getting their aid. This is of course black magic and it involves calling up and having converse with the followers of Satan, those who had rebelled with him and been cast out of Heaven with him. It was this forbidden art that Faust practised and which led to both his pact with Satan and his ultimate damnation.

During the Renaissance the attitude of the Church to ritual magic was conflicted. In theory there were forms of magic that were compatible with Christianity, as argued by one of the earliest advocates, Pico Della Mirandola. However, there was always the feeling that relying upon spiritual powers to achieve ends in this world was both dangerous and incompatible with Christian doctrine. This view rapidly became the predominant one among Protestants in particular, for a simple reason. A core feature of Reformed Christianity was its rejection of the undoubted magical elements of medieval Catholicism, such as relics, miracles and intercessions performed by saints after the Apostolic age, and the highly ritualised liturgy. These were seen as pagan elements that had crept into and corrupted the Church so the rejection of ideas and practices that actually came from pagan antiquity was all the fiercer. For almost all Protestant thinkers magic of all kinds was at best superstition, more likely the work of the Devil. The contradiction in this way of thinking was that the magic was supposedly both fraudulent and yet effective and dangerous. Tying it all to the Devil squared that circle since it was his power that made it effective and yet since it came from the Father of Lies it did not bring the benefits it promised. Among Roman Catholics there was initially greater sympathy for forms of Christianity that drew upon esoteric idea systems such as Hermeticism but latterly the Church turned against it. One key event was the execution of the Catholic Hermetic thinker Giordano Bruno in 1600. One legacy of Hermeticism was the elaboration and working out of a cosmology and set of theories about the nature of things such as matter and energy that drew on ancient and medieval thought but made them far more complex, creating a vast and comprehensive picture of the universe. There was significant overlap with ideas that went on to be important in modern science, in the work of Bruno for example but also in the thought of people more associated with science such as Kepler and Newton. The Devil in one form or another had a prominent part in this new or amended 'world picture'.

The thing that clearly marked off some forms of ritual magic as Satanic was the use of ritual to summon and bind and then employ fallen spirits and allies of the Devil. There were attempts to give this a Christian covering by making the rituals ones in which the demons were subordinated to the magician and made tools of his will by the use of biblical quotes and the use of the divine names, often drawing on the myths surrounding the Biblical King Solomon (See Chapter 7 for more details). This was though window dressing of a transparent kind. What the elaborate textbooks of magic produced during the Renaissance did was to add another element to the image of the Devil, which was the details of the infernal hierarchy he presided over. In the Middle Ages he was thought of as a kind of counter-monarch, a dark counterpart to both the heavenly monarchy of God and its earthly counterparts. The subordinate hierarchy though was thought of in much less detail. In the Renaissance this was filled in, with an entire aristocracy of Hell being worked out. The Devil now became someone with an array of helpers, as remarked earlier so that he now became the centre of a web or society of demons, evil spirits, and magical creatures of various kinds. This was an important addition to the mythology, so much so that it gets two chapters of its own. This was an area that had dramatic real-life effects as it led to the massive witch-hunt of the sixteenth and seventeenth centuries, something that would actually be repeated in much more recent times.

The visual arts and literature show these changes in how the devil was imagined and reflect the greater importance and prominence that he came to have in both intellectual thought and popular belief. He appears in the many works of demonology and witch-hunting that were produced at this time and in the works of theology that the reformation and Counter-Reformation produced in such quantity. In literature works such as Marlowe's *Doctor Faustus* show the shift to a more spiritualised understanding of his nature. It is the visual arts where the shift is most clear. In earlier works such as those of Durer he is still monstrous and bestial. In the work of many of the artists of this period there is a distinct shift in representations of matters such as Satan and Hell in which he is still shown as monstrous and grotesque but now with a definite element of the surreal and fantastic. This is most obvious in the well-known works of Hieronymus Bosch and Pieter Breughel but it is a feature of many other fifteenth and sixteenth century artists' work, such as those of Lukas or Frans Cranach. As time passed the Devil became more human in appearance until by the mid seventeenth century and the works of painters such as Signorelli, he has become fully humanised with only distorted features such as wings to indicate who he is.

In the two hundred and fifty years of the Renaissance there was probably more interest in and concern with the Devil and his doings than at any time before or since. Many were concerned and alarmed by his power and capacity, some were intrigued and fascinated by them. He became a great concern for theologians, philosophers and thinkers, in a different way to the interest that their Medieval predecessors had had in him. As a result of all of this exploration and the many accounts of his doings that were produced his personality and character took on a more detailed quality and he became the darky cynical and amusing, charming yet malevolent and sinister person that we are still familiar with. His appearance became different, more courtly and less bestial, reflecting the new-found emphasis on his aristocratic and princely nature and persona. He became more active and powerful, with great influence in both the material and human worlds and in the deepest recesses of people's minds and feelings, as they became more aware of him. His power was enhanced by his being given an army of helpers and deputies, all devoted to his cause and he was now located in an elaborate society and political order of his own, set against both earthly rule and divine authority. Finally, he became associated with an elaborate system of thought and ideas and a worked-out cosmology and mechanics that gave the understanding of him a magical as well as a theological aspect. This launched him into a new career, in the modern world, in which although his existence was often denied he continued to exist in a kind of counter-tradition or learning. In this new world that succeeded the Renaissance the new form he had taken then became the subject of a slow but definite process of re-evaluation.

Further Reading
Brock, Michelle D., Raiswell, Richard, Winter, David R. (eds.) (2018) *Knowing Demons, Knowing Spirits in the Early Modern Period*. Palgrave.

Butler, Elizabeth M. (1998, 1st published 1949) *Ritual Magic*. Sutton.

Butler, Elizabeth M. (1998, 1st published 1952) *The Fortunes of Faust*. Sutton.

Clark, Stuart (1997) *Thinking With Demons: The Idea of Witchcraft in Early Modern Europe.* Oxford University Press

Collins, David J. (ed.) (2018) *The Cambridge History of Magic and Witchcraft in the West From Antiquity to the Present.* Cambridge University Press.

Goodrick-Clarke, Nicholas (2008). *The Western Esoteric Traditions: A Historical Introduction.* Oxford University Press.

Gosden, Chris (2020) *The History of Magic: from Alchemy to Witchcraft, from the Ice Age to the Present.* Penguin

Katz, David S. (2005) *The Occult Tradition: From the Renaissance to the Present Day.* Jonathan Cape.

Muchembled, Robert (2003). *A History of the Devil from the Middle Ages to the Present.* Polity Press.

Oldridge, Darren (2000) *The Devil in Early Modern England.* Sutton.

Raiswell, Richard & Dandle, Peter (eds.) (2012) *The Devil in Society in Pre-Modern Europe.* Cambridge University Press.

Robinson, Daniel (ed) 2018 *The History of Evil in the Early Modern Age 1450–1700.* Routledge.

Russell, Jeffrey Burton (1986). *Mephistopheles: The Devil in the Modern World.* Cornell University Press.

Seligman, Kurt (2018) *The Mirror of Magic: A History of Magic in the Western World.* Inner Traditions.

Walden, Justine (2015) "The Devil in the Renaissance, or, Diabolizing the Political in Fifteenth Century Florence" *Renaissance Society of America Annual Meeting,* Berlin March 26–28. https://www.academia.edu/15704169/The_Devil_in_the_Renaissance_or_Diabolizing_the_Political_in_Fifteenth_Century_Florence_Renaissance_Society_of_America_Annual_Meeting_Berlin_26_28_March_2015

Whitehead, Willis F. (ed.) (2006 1st published 1897) *Agrippa's Occult Philosophy: Natural Magic.* Dover.

Chapter 5. The Devil in the Modern World

The easy assumption about the Devil's place in modernity would be that he has gradually faded away, as belief in his existence declines and reason comes to dominate the intellectual world in place of religion. This though would be a serious mistake. The modern age is actually one of paradox where the Devil is concerned. On the one hand these certainly has been a decline in belief in his existence and in the importance of the part he plays in mainstream Christian thinking and theology. On the other hand, he has not simply disappeared from view, or moved into the category of the fabulous or fantastic. There is a stubborn persistence of belief in his reality and existence, from a surprisingly wide range of people. Latterly there has been a revival of interest in him or at least in the idea of him, as a way of understanding things that the dominant ideas of our times cannot come to grips with. The other feature of the Devil in the modern world is the way the evaluation of him has undergone a radical revision, as far as many are concerned. In an interesting and ironic process (given its origins) the dramatic and alluring persona he came to have during the Renaissance has turned in some quarters into positive approbation. There has even been most recently the appearance of an actual religion in which he is the central, and venerated figure. Simultaneously there are plenty of warnings about his menace, leading in one case to a judicial tragedy. Meanwhile he has come to occupy a prominent position in popular culture of all kinds.

The first two thirds of the seventeenth century in Europe saw the climax of the religious fervour that had followed the Renaissance and found expression in the Reformation and Counter-Reformation. This was the century of religious wars, culminating in the horrors of the Thirty Years War of 1618–48, which laid waste Germany. It was also the time when the savage witch-hunts of the time reached a climax in many parts of Europe and the fear of the Devil and his machinations was more intense than at any other time since his emergence. He loomed larger and more menacingly in the imagination of people then than at any time before or since. By the latter years of the century Europe entered a period of exhaustion in many ways. Thinking people were weary of the religious passions of the previous two hundred years and the terrible consequences they had brought. From the 1690s onwards we can observe a turning away from the passionate certainties of the past. The devout turned increasingly to personal and private piety and holiness while others became sceptics or adopted a way of thinking that while still Christian was milder and gentler than that of the era now passed. From Spinoza onwards we can observe the appearance of freethinking deism (believing in God but not a particular revealed religion) and even outright atheism. This was still something that would get you into trouble but it became increasingly common, whereas in the sixteenth or early seventeenth century it was almost impossible to not be a believer in revealed religion, because otherwise the world did not make sense.

The shorthand way of describing this is to say that in the eighteenth century, Europe entered an Age of Reason in which the beliefs and claims of revealed religion progressively lost their hold on the minds of Europeans, initially many of the educated elite but increasingly those further down the scale as well. Alongside this was a decline in the other system of systematic thought that had dominated the Renaissance, that of ritual magic. What happened was the rise of the way of thinking that went on to become hegemonic in the modern world, that of modern science. Initially this was a part of the magical tradition and grew out of it but by the early eighteenth century it had become distinct. The key event was the publication of Newton's *Principia* in 1681 as that created a way of understanding the world and natural phenomena that did not involve the actions of spirits or the continuing intervention of the deity. That event though illustrates how initially magic and science were intertwined for, as we have known since the 1930s, Newton was as much a magician and occultist as he was a modern scientist. In the modern world, as the philosopher Charles Taylor observed recently, religion and magic lost their once preeminent role in understanding and making sense of the world. They still exist, as we will see, but they were increasingly marginal ways of explaining things as that function was taken over by science.

As science became increasingly the lens through which the world was seen and understood, so religious conceptions became less important. One of these was that of the Devil. Over the last two centuries he became far less important for the way educated people made sense of the world, but there was also a decline in his place in mainstream religious thought. Thus, in mainstream Christian theology there has been a steady decline in his importance. A key factor was the emergence of the 'higher criticism' in Germany in the middle part of the nineteenth century. This was a method of forensic analysis of texts using philology, which was applied to the biblical texts. The result was to reveal the historical process of assembling and compiling supposedly divinely inspired scriptures and in that process to deconstruct much of the traditional interpretations and understandings of various Biblical narratives. One of these was the story of Satan and his role that had been worked out or put together in the time of Late Antiquity. The outcome was that most theologians came to reject the idea of the Devil as an actual person or entity. He became thought of instead as a personification of the dark side and urges of the human mind and personality or of human nature more generally. As a symbol or way of understanding human psychology he became a less central figure and above all he became less of an actor in the story. The idea of an actual physical Devil or of a being that could take physical form became a marginal one, rejected by the great majority of theologians.

The rise of science as a way of understanding the world also reduced the centrality of the Devil and his actions as a way of explaining human actions or events in the natural world. Because narratives involving him or claims about his doings could not meet the canons of proof employed in science, they were relegated to the categories of superstition or mythology and as the scientific way of understanding the world became the dominant one for most people by the later nineteenth century so the Devil moved into the realm of superstition or fantasy as far as the general culture was concerned. This meant he was still a subject of interest even of fascination but he was no longer the fearsome or threatening and subversive character he had been previously. One reflection of this is the way he progressively became a figure of light-hearted fun in much popular culture – people do not make jokes of that kind about something they believe in and take seriously. Interestingly while belief in the personal Devil declines in modernity, even amongst Christians, belief in a personal God has had much greater staying power. It seems that while many became sceptical of the notion of a supernatural source of evil, they remained open to that of a supernatural source of good. One reason for this was the increasing prevalence of the idea that the world and humans were naturally good and so bad things were caused by human failure or ill-will, which could be identified, countered and corrected.

However, as always, there is another side to this story. Although religion (meaning mainly Christianity in this context) has lost its place as the predominant way of thinking about the world it has not vanished. Over the three centuries since 1700 there have been a series of revivals or resurgences of both Christian belief and organised religion (reawakenings in the American parlance). This was particularly noticeable in the nineteenth century and by 1881 in Britain religious observance in Britain (as measured by things like church attendance and denominational membership, as recorded in the census) was at an all-time high and certainly higher than it had been a hundred years earlier. Outside Europe active Christianity continues to spread, particularly in Africa. Islam has experienced a resurgence in the last fifty years, similar to the one experienced by Christianity in the mid to late nineteenth century in Europe and in the 1950s in the United States. The persistence of religion as a force in social life means that ideas that are a historic part of the monotheistic faiths are still part of the mental world of most people, even if the belief is less literal than before.

Even that last point needs to be qualified however. As mainstream Christianity gave ground to the higher criticism or incorporated its findings into its theology, so there was a reaction against that process. The most prominent form of this was fundamentalism, a term derived from a collection of twelve volumes published in 1910 in the United States and entitled *The Fundamentals*. Fundamentals in this context meant doctrines and teachings or understandings of scripture that were fundamental to the faith so that if they were denied or altered a theology or church could no longer be seen as a true continuation of historic Christianity. One of those doctrines was that of the real existence and personality of the Devil. This only had one piece about it in the twelve volumes but references to him appeared throughout the whole set. Fundamentalism became the term for a kind of Christianity that rejected theological modernism and its compromises with modernity and instead asserted a doctrine derived in great part from a strict Biblical literalism. Although a reaction against modernism in theology it was itself a modern phenomenon, partly because the stress on literalism meant the rejection of a large part of historical exegesis and hermeneutic. It became a vibrant and successful form of Christianity and dominant in a number of denominations, particularly in the United States and also elsewhere. It is often associated with evangelical Protestantism and the original volumes contained several pieces denying that 'Romanism' should be considered a variant of Christianity but there was and is an equivalent in Roman Catholicism. There are of course similar types of movement in both Judaism and Islam.

This means that the idea of a personal and real Devil as an important element of belief remained alive and well for many believers, even if mainstream churches have moved away from it. An interest in the power and activity of Satan in the world became important for many fundamentalist denominations as the twentieth century progressed and not only in the United States. This played out in things like the Satanic Panic described later in Chapter 8 and it led to the production of many tracts and handbooks concerned with identifying and countering the machinations of Satan. This is actually rising in importance as a belief in practising Christianity for a simple reason: over the last hundred years the proportion of all self-described Christians who adhere to some form of fundamentalist theology has increased, partly because they tend to have more children than the norm and also because mainstream religion has suffered losses to secularism and alternative kinds of belief such as New Age ones. Bertrand Russel (an ardent atheist of course) was fond of saying that Christianity was a religion that had lost its nerve: fundamentalist Christianity has not lost its nerve. Moreover, most of the rapid growth of Christianity in Africa has been led by evangelical fundamentalist denominations and even the followers of mainstream ones such as Anglicanism or Catholicism in Africa are far more likely to be theological conservatives than is the case in Europe or North America, and consequently to believe in a personal Devil. In Africa itself many traditional folk beliefs about magic and spirits have been carried over by converts and just as in Europe at an earlier date these have been attached to the figure of Satan. Thus, traditional notions about witch craft and possession by spirits have been reinterpreted using the ideas of witchcraft and the demonic that have been associated with Satan since the later Middle Ages. Meanwhile, many traditional Islamic beliefs, including those in Iblis and other evil djinni (spiritual beings and powers) are enjoying a new lease of life.

This means that the traditional beliefs about the Devil and his nature as they had come to be held by the seventeenth century are still alive and well in the modern world. They are now a minority tradition and also not found among the elites of society but they are nonetheless widespread and are actually becoming more so with time. Another belief that has survived and even enjoyed a revival despite the general trend of the modern world towards rationalism and materialism is that in magic – or magick as it is now usually called. This has persisted throughout modern history as a kind of counter-tradition to that of scientific rationalism, existing below the surface and in the shadows of modern culture but still influential and becoming visible in surprising times and places. As the Devil had come to be strongly associated with this during the Renaissance so he continues to play a leading part in this counter-tradition or rebel subculture.

In the eighteenth century as science and the Enlightenment increased in influence, magic became an object of derision as far as most intellectuals were concerned. It was seen as an example of backwardness, part of the dark age that the Enlightenment was an escape from. Just as a reaction against the religious enthusiasm and fanaticism of the sixteenth and seventeenth centuries had been one of the drivers of the turn to rationalism, so was revulsion from the atrocities of the witch mania and the fear of magic and spiritual darkness that had driven it. As the persecution of those accused of witchcraft came to be seen as a barbarous relic of ignorance, so the associated belief in magic, demons, and satanic pacts was put into that category. Nevertheless, the tradition of magic survived. At a folk level it was as persistent and widespread as ever in the shape of charms, rituals and beliefs about luck and fortune. What also survived was systematic ritual and theoretical magic. As explained, this had been closely connected to the early forms of sciences such as astronomy and chemistry and we could well say that science grew out of ritual magic. By the late seventeenth century, in the writings of people like Robert Boyle, science had become a clearly defined and distinct way of thinking that was defined in great part in opposition or contrast to formal magic.

Some though remained committed to systematic magic as a way of both understanding the world and manipulating it. One such was a man called Francis Barrett, who in 1801 published a work called *The Magus or Celestial Intelligencer*. This was not an original work but an eclectic compendium of extracts from Renaissance works of ceremonial and natural magic, particularly the *Four Books of Occult Philosophy* of Agrippa. What Barrett did was to organise these extracts in a way that made it more of a practical 'how to do it' handbook. As we shall see the work went on to have a considerable influence subsequently. Eighteenth century occultism as found across Europe had four main aspects. The first was the transmission but amendment of Renaissance hermeticism and associated magical disciplines such as astrology and alchemy and also alongside them ritual magic and evocation of spirits, including dark or fallen ones. Barrett's work was an example of this. The second was fortune telling and predictions of the future, particularly methods involving either contact with spirits or the use of the tarot cards. This last was introduced in its modern form by the French writer Antoine Court de Gebelen. The third was an area where magic still overlapped with science in the shape of theories and practices that were taken seriously by some at the time but later relegated to the category of pseudo-science. The most important of these was mesmerism, a theory and associated technique developed by the German thinker Franz Mesmer. Today he is associated with the practice of hypnotism but his central idea was that of a vital force or natural magnetism (as he called it) found in both living creatures and inanimate objects. The fourth was mystical Christianity of a particular type that drew upon the Hermetic tradition. This found expression in movements such as Rosicrucianism and some types of Freemasonry, particularly the esoteric form of Christianity known as Martinism, after its founder Louis-Claude de Saint-Martin.

So alongside or even overlapping the Enlightenment and the growth of modern science was a kind of counter-tradition of occult theory and practice which existed physically as a series of thinkers and teachers who transmitted the ideas and developed them. Despite the views of the more traditional minded Christians the Devil as understood in classic Christian tradition was not a feature. He did figure in it though, in a different way. The core ideas uniting all of the four aspects of modern occultism was and is the notion firstly that the world is full of and even animated by, spiritual beings and forces and secondly of the efficacy of ritual practices and the knowledge they embody to control or use those spiritual forces to bring about physical changes (such as ensuring health or wealth) and also to predict the future. The Devil plays a part in this way of thinking in two ways. The first is that he, and the entire infernal hierarchy, are seen as simply one of the categories or types of spiritual forces that exist and can be used. He and they are dangerous and hostile in the way that certain natural phenomena or creatures are but controllable. Crucially they are not malevolent as in the traditional Christian conception of them.

In other words, in esoteric and occult thought there is still an idea of a being or entity who is identified with many of the traditional features of the Devil as they were held by the Renaissance, but with much of the theological framework removed or radically altered. There is a move back to monism and the belief in a world with an ultimate and single divine power that has a light and a dark side or which manifests itself in both ways. (The two sides are also identified with right and left, hence the talk of right- and left-hand paths or ways to knowledge). In intellectual history this way of thinking became more prominent in the eighteenth and nineteenth century in Europe as a result of three sources or influences. These were ideas from Hinduism (where monism is a common idea) due to greater contact between Europe and India; the persistence and development of hermetic ideas that had entered European intellectual life during the Renaissance; and the influence of Jewish mysticism or Kabbalah. This had also entered the mental world of Christian Europeans in the later fifteenth and early sixteenth century, although the ideas themselves are much older.

It was the third of these that mainly gave the Devil a firm location and role in the modern occult counter-tradition. In Kabbalah there is a single divine power and the universe is seen as an emanation from it. The emanation happens through ten aspects of the divine, the Sephiroth (divine lights). Some of these (the right-hand side) manifest as benign others (the left-hand side) as harsh and violent. This is represented in a diagram, the Tree of Life, with the ten Sephiroth nodes connected by a network of 22 paths. Each of the paths is identified with one of the Major Arcana of the Tarot deck. In this, the Devil is a way of personalising and thinking about aspects of the dark, left-hand side of the creation, and the values associated with it and he is also a spiritual power or force that can be used in various ways by the adept or magus. He is dangerous but naturally, in the way that electricity is.

The second way that the Devil played a part in the modern occult tradition was as a benign or admirable figure. This was something truly novel, a reversal or radical amendment of the core concept. This grows out of the wider movement of the modern and its rejection of the traditional but it also has a specific and direct source. This was the widespread reaction to or reading of one of the greatest literary representations of Satan, which has shaped the modern image of him more than anything else. This was, of course, John Milton's *Paradise Lost*. The way this came to be read and the actual influence it had on many people is a classic case of the difference between the intent of an author as regards the meaning of a text and the meaning ascribed to it by its readers. Milton's purpose in writing his great epic poem was, as he himself put it, to justify the ways of God to Man. However, the portrayal of Satan in the work (discussed in more detail in Chapter 10) was read by many in a way that he had not intended. For many readers Satan became an admirable figure, at least an anti-hero, maybe the actual hero of the work. He was indomitable, defiant, daring, charismatic and a leader. Above all he was a rebel, who asserted his own judgment and identity. That this reading should become widespread so soon after Milton wrote the poem (as found in the works of William Blake for example) is symptomatic of a whole array of cultural and psychological shifts that took place at that time, initially in Europe.

In Milton's account the thing Satan does that leads to his rebellion, fall, and defeat is that he denies the nature of God and his attributes, above all his omnipotence. After he is cast into Hell in Book One, he delivers a famous oration that many have found inspiring, concluding with the ringing declaration *"To reign is worth ambition, though in Hell. Better to reign in Hell than serve in Heaven"*. In Milton's original intention this shows that Satan simply doesn't get it. God is all powerful so no matter what Satan does he ultimately ends up serving God's purpose. His corruption of Adam and Eve is not a victory because it simply leads to the greatest possible act of goodness, the redemptive life and death of the Son. Very soon after Milton wrote his work readers came to see Satan's attitude and character as admirable because it was a rejection of authority and an assertion of individuality, self-will, and free judgment – of individual independence and autonomy. That this reading was even possible shows that a profound subterranean cultural shift had happened. In a very real sense the emergent modern culture, like Satan, denied that God was God in the way Milton and earlier thinkers had imagined him. Rebellion and resistance to authority had become for many something to admire. This was linked to two central features of modernity, individualism and innovation. Individualism in that the autonomous person or subject had become the way human beings increasingly thought of themselves – or was what they aspired to. Innovation because questioning authority and tradition was obviously linked with that. For a succession of figures in the modern world of the last three centuries the Devil as the greatest of all rebels is certainly a figure with positive and heroic qualities even if he is still seen as ultimately malign, while for some he becomes an actual positive figure.

One of the specific features of this revaluation appears in the later eighteenth and early nineteenth century and is the second way that the Devil comes to be a presence in the world of the counter-tradition. He becomes for many the source of reason, knowledge and innovation. This identification had always been there in fact, what changed was the evaluation of the elements. One of his features, originating in the Middle Ages but becoming much more prominent in the Renaissance was that he had enormous knowledge, which he would share for a price. The association of formal knowledge with the demonic went back even further though. In *Genesis* the various arts of civilisation are associated with the descendants of Cain, the first murderer. In the apocryphal works such as *Enoch* in which the story of the Watchers is developed the rebel angels are said to have taught all kinds of techniques and forbidden knowledge to humanity – this as much as lusting after human women and abandoning their posts was the essence of their rebellion.

The usual name for the positive view of the Devil in modernity as a source of liberating knowledge is Luciferianism. In this the Devil is referred to by the name he bore before his rebellion and fall in the traditional Christian account, that of Lucifer. Translated literally this means the light bringer. In this way of thinking, Lucifer the rebel angel is a Prometheus figure who defies God to bring knowledge and reason to humanity. He is a rebel angel but a benign one who brings benefits to humanity. He is also associated with free thinking, personal independence, rationality and worship of the self. As in the Medieval and Renaissance myth of the Magus, the goal is supposed to be self-mastery and realisation, and the elevation of the self as an object of veneration to a god-like status. There is thus an association with individualism and ethical egoism. Over the last three hundred years there have been several organised movements devoted to this understanding of the Devil. According to some, it is the underlying belief of Freemasonry, or at least its more radical variants. Freemasons themselves have always denied this – the problem for them is the existence of organisations that do espouse the idea and which make use of Masonic rituals, terms, and symbols but which are not, and never have been, recognised or approved of by any Grand Lodge.

One very specific form that this identification of the Devil with freethought and enlightenment took and continues to take is the philosophy and practice of libertinism. In popular usage this just means sexual promiscuity and indulging in physical pleasure with no moral or ethical limits – a libertine is a person who does this. The term actually has a deeper meaning though, and refers to a theory of ethics and a model of how to live one's life. It has been advocated by a number of prominent or notorious figures and actually practiced by organised groups, most notably in the eighteenth century. The basic idea of libertinism is that you should do whatever you chose. This is captured in the core principle "Do what you will". The expression comes from the sixteenth century work *Gargantua and Pantagruel*, by Francois Rabelais and in that work is the rule (the only rule in fact) for a parodic monastic community, the Abbey of Theleme. The key term is 'will'. To follow the principle of "Do what you will' does not mean to act out every casual impulse or desire. It means to follow through on conscious and deliberate choice or desires, expressions of the will, the active and choosing part of the mind. Since each person has their own will this is a radically egoistic and individualist principle. It means that nobody's will should be subject to that of another. It also means that things such as explicit laws and also rules, traditions, social norms, and moral codes are rejected as constraints on the exercise of the will, even if they are obeyed for prudential reasons. The idea is that by living this way the practitioner achieves true self-mastery and self-realisation (as well as having a good time). The secondary principle is hedonism, that physical and earthly pleasure is good and desirable and should be pursued. In particular sexual pleasure is elevated both as an end in itself and as a means to achieving an elevated state of consciousness. Libertinism can take two forms: predatory in which exercising power over others is allowed (so a philosophy of 'might makes right') and consensual in which all wills are given equal respect (so that relations and fulfilling of the will have to be consensual).

In the eighteenth-century libertine ideas were expressed in a number of bestselling novels that combined eroticism with philosophy, such as *Therese the Philosopher*, and *The Indiscreet Jewels* by Dennis Diderot. The best known or most infamous are the works of the Marquis de Sade such as *Juliette*, and *The 120 Days of Sodom*. In several of these the Devil is freely alluded to as an example of the principle of libertinism. The whole genre and the underlying philosophy were both described and criticised by Laclos in 1782 in his masterpiece, *Les Liasons Dangereuses*. There were others who not only read books but put the philosophy into practice in private clubs. The best known of these was the Hellfire

Club. This name was given to several clubs or associations over the course of the eighteenth century, all of them devoted to the exploration of debauchery of various kinds. The best known was the one set up by the politician and rake Sir Francis Dashwood in 1746 under the title (adopted later) of The Order of the Friars of St Francis of Wycombe (although it went under other similar names as well such as The Monks of Medmenham). The motto and rule of the Club was the aforementioned "Do What You Will".

The meetings took place initially at Medmenham Abbey, near to Dashwood's estate at West Wycombe and subsequently moved to a series of caves on the estate. The meetings by all accounts involved both a wide variety of sexual goings on and blasphemous parodies of the Mass, involving veneration of Satan (blasphemy and eroticism being combined when prostitutes hired for the occasion were dressed up as nuns). The part played by allusions to the Devil in these kinds of goings on was both playful and serious: playful because what was happening was not serious devil-worship but serious because the deliberate blasphemy and invocation of Satan was meant to signify a complete rejection of traditional Christianity – at least for the elite. Dashwood's club was one of a number of such organisations, another well-known one was the Beggar's Benison (or to give its full title The Most Ancient and Most Puissant Order of the Beggar's Benison and Merryland, Antruther) founded in Scotland, which existed from 1739 to 1836. Here the parodic Satanism was not such an element with the focus being on sexual libertinism and initiation rituals involving mutual masturbation.

The connection between sexual libertinism and both occultism and dark magic is one that continues to the present day. Sexual rituals of various kinds and acts that are intended to build up and intensify sexual feelings are an important part of many magical rites. The reasons are twofold. Firstly, because this creates an intense and powerful feeling or passion on the part of the practitioner – the aim is to control or channel it so as to achieve magical effects. This is a practical reason. The second, and the reason for the continued association of these kinds of practice with dark magic and the Devil, is their transgressive nature – they are part of a repudiation of orthodox ethics and morality and an assertion of an alternative of self-mastery and personal liberation. They are also pleasurable and we may suspect that in some cases the ritual is just the excuse or pretext for the orgy.

These various ideas, of ritual magic, pseudo-science (or forbidden knowledge as it was often presented as being), predicting the future and influencing the world by occult means, occult rationalism, and libertinism all enjoyed a sustained revival from the middle decades of the nineteenth century onwards. An additional element that entered the mix at that time was a series of revivals of pre-Christian paganism, particularly Celtic and Germanic. Barrett's *Magus* became a significant influence on or starting point for this, because of its influence on two of the key figures in the occult revival, the English author and politician Sir Edward Bulwer-Lytton, and the French occultist Eliphas Levi. The former wrote several occult themed novels in his large oeuvre but his main role was as a connector or facilitator. Levi, as explained in Chapter 9, was the person who systematised ritual magic in the form that is known today, drawing on *The Magus* and other formal works. By the end of the nineteenth and the early part of the twentieth century occultism had become a major feature of the culture of the fin de siècle with a range of associated phenomena such as spiritualism, Theosophy, New Thought, and a variety of neo-pagan movements. Some of the latter in the Germanic parts of Europe had a role (significant but also greatly exaggerated) in the ideology of the Nazi Party, in the shape of the system of ideas known as ariosophism. Satan became an important figure in two artistic movements of that period, Decadence and Symbolism (often conflated though actually distinct). Both are usually seen as starting with the work of the French poet Baudelaire, particularly his *Fleurs Du Mal*. Outright Satanism and black magic featured prominently in one of the best known of Decadent literary works, *La-Bas* by Joris Karl Huysmans.

One of the major organisations of that time was the Hermetic Order of the Golden Dawn, which had a number of prominent and distinguished members, such as W B Yeats. As set out in Chapter 9 it was through this that Aleister Crowley entered the world of occultism. He proved to be an enormously influential figure with the counter-tradition and it was through him and the system of ritual magic he created, known as Thelemic magic (after the abbey in Rabelais) that the idea of using dark spirits evoked in rituals became a definite element in it. His work *Magick in Theory and Practice* is the main theoretical text in contemporary ritual magic (now usually styled 'magick' in Crowley's style to distinguish it from 'magic' which is used to refer to conjuring and illusion working). The American offshoot of Crowley's organisation was the indirect origin (as described in more detail later) of the contemporary phenomenon of explicit and organised Satanism. This is in some ways the culmination of the revaluation of the Devil, from a malevolent adversary to a neutral but dangerous spiritual force to a positive one, to an actual object of veneration or even worship. The most widespread type of modern Satanism, founded by Anton LaVey and named after him, is actually a type of atheism – we might describe it as atheism with attitude – but there is also theistic satanism.

So, belief in the Devil may have been undermined by modern rationalism and science but he, or the idea of him, has proved to be extremely persistent. He has survived and even flourished, while the way he is understood has also mutated further to the point where he has become a positive figure for some. As explained in later chapters, as official belief in him has declined so the interest in him on the part of authors and artists has grown. He is a major protagonist in a range of works of literature ranging from pulp fiction to modern classics such as *The Brothers Karamazov* and *The Master and Margerita*. He features in many visual arts and has become prominent is some forms of popular music, particularly so-called heavy metal. There is also a long list of films that feature him, openly or allusively. This persistence in popular culture come from two contrasting sources. On the one side, the decline in the near universal belief in a powerful and personal Devil that had gripped Renaissance Europe means that he can be treated more lightly and so he comes to be a figure in popular fiction and even advertising. As Robert Muchembled points out, part of this comes from the way that things once seen as sinful or questionable such as physical pleasure, particularly sexual, are now seen as objects to be pursued and good (Muchembled, 2003). The association of these things with the traditional symbol of the Devil is a lighthearted way of giving them the faintest frisson of still being forbidden fruits. The change in the way many of the things once associated with Satan are viewed is most clear in the case of witchcraft where the once-feared and dreaded practice has become a semi-respectable New Religion. This has started to happen even with dark creatures such as vampires and werewolves (though not yet with zombies!).

The Devil also though acts as a symbol, of evil and malice, even if people no longer believe in his literal existence. The other side of the story is that there is still a need to account for and explain egregious acts of evil and cruelty and in particular ones that seem to have no motivation other than malice – or are seen as such (not the same thing of course). The decline in the influence of traditional theology has arguably left modern societies unable to understand or come to terms with the human capacity for wickedness and cruelty. Acts of that kind now seem incomprehensible and baffling, incompatible with the way being human is commonly understood. This is shown in the way serial killers or people who kill children are commonly described as 'monsters', with the implication that they are not human. One response is to use the Devil as a symbolic representation of the dark side of human nature and the human mind and to use that as a way of explaining things such as the Holocaust or the Gulag or the genocide in Rwanda. The difficulty with this is that it leads to a very dark and ultimately pessimistic view of human nature and can lead to people who actually have complex and bad but understandable motives being presented and thought of as moved by pure spite and desire to destroy the good. In that case there is no point in understanding what motivates them, much less talking to them, the only thing to do is to kill or capture them. Sometimes this is necessary but this approach can actually make it more difficult to deal with phenomena such as terrorism and political violence, or prejudice, or to actually understand what is going on in the mind of psychopaths and predators.

The third alternative is to actually believe in an external Devil. He may be an actual person or he may be thought of again as symbolic, representing the malign or dangerous forces that exist outside the individual and in the world. As explained earlier the old Renaissance idea of an active and powerful personal Devil is still alive and well in the sub-culture of evangelical fundamentalism. This again however, can have bad results as the panics described in Chapter 8 show. Not all mainstream theologians have given up on the Devil however. There are people like the philosopher Gordon Graham who have argued forcefully for this and there are theologians in all three major Christian traditions (Roman Catholic, Reformed, and Orthodox) who still uphold it, including two recent Popes. This can take the form of belief in an actual supernatural and spiritual entity but it can also take the form of a belief of a principle or force of evil that is found outside the individual and manifests itself in events, objects, practices and institutions, often of an everyday nature. This is the kind of explanation for the evil of the Holocaust and other genocides or acts of mass slaughter put forward by people like Primo Levi and Robert Conquest. As Darren Oldridge observes this way of thinking is close to the older idea of the Devil as the Prince of this World and it makes the point that temptation is an inherent feature of everyday experience that anyone can succumb to and which can lead ordinary people, particularly in large numbers, to do truly terrible things (Oldridge, 2012). The Devil may have been softened or transformed by the processes of modernity but it may be that as a feature of a world that is inherently tragic and flawed, he is inescapable.

Further Reading

Ashe, Geoffrey (2000) *The Hell-Fire Clubs: A History of Anti-Morality*. Sutton.

Barrett, Francis (2000, 1st published. 1801) *The Magus, or Celestial Intelligencer: A Complete System of Occult Philosophy*. Weiser Books.

Black, Candice (2006) *Satanica Sexualis: An Encyclopedia of Sex and the Devil*. Wet Angel.

Dan, Joseph (2007) *Kabbalah: A Very Short Introduction*. Oxford University Press.

Davies, Owen (1999) *Witchcraft, Magic and Culture 1736–1951*. Manchester University Press

De Blecourt, William, Hutton, Ronald, and La Fontaine, Jean (1999) *The Athlone History of Witchcraft and Magic in Europe Volume 6: The Twentieth Century*. Athlone Press.

Drury, Nevill (2000) *The History of Magic in the Modern Age: A Quest for Personal Transformation*. Constable.

Gellman, Jerome (ed.) (2018) *The History of Evil from the Mid-Twentieth century to Today 1950–2018*. Routledge.

Gijswijt-Hofstra, Marijke, Levack, Brian P., and Porter, Roy (1999) *The Athlone History of Witchcraft and Magic in Europe Volume 5: The Eighteenth and Nineteenth Centuries*. Athlone Press.

Greer, John Michael (2017) *The Occult Book: A Chronological Journey from Alchemy to Wicca*. Sterling.

Harrison, Victoria S. (ed.) (2018) *The History of Evil in the Early Twentieth Century 1900–1950*. Routledge.

Hedley, Douglas (ed.) (2018) *The History of Evil in the Eighteenth and Nineteenth Centuries 1700–1900*. Routledge.

Hunter, Michael (2020) *The Decline of Magic: Britain in the Enlightenment*. Yale University Press.

Josephson – Storm, Jason A. (2017) *The Myth of Disenchantment: Magic, Modernity and the Birth of the Human Sciences*. University of Chicago Press.

King, Francis X. (1992) *The Flying Sorcerer: Being the Magical and Aeronautical Adventures of Francis Barrett, Author of The Magus*. Mandrake Books

Lord, Evelyn (2008) *The Hell-Fire Clubs: Sex, Satanism and Secret Societies*. Yale University Press

Owen, Alex (2004) *The Place of Enchantment: British Occultism and the Culture of the Modern*. University of Chicago Press.

Russell, Jeffrey Burton (1986). *Mephistopheles: The Devil in the Modern World*. Cornell University Press.

Schreck, Nikolas & Zeena (2002) *Demons of the Flesh: The Complete Guide to Sex Magic*. Creation Books.

Tucker, Robert C. (1999) *An Age For Lucifer: Predatory Spirituality and The Quest For Godhood*. Holmes Publishing Group.

Waters, Thomas (2019). *Cursed Britain: A History of Witchcraft and Black Magic in Modern Times*. Yale University Press.

Weir, David (2018) *Decadence: A Very Short Introduction*. Oxford University Press.

Chapter 6. The Devil's Residence: Hell

Although the Devil as a spiritual power is present everywhere in this world, he also has a particular location or abode, his own domain and stronghold which is at the same time his prison. This of course is Hell. Just as the idea of the Devil is an aspect of the monotheistic religions rather than all religious traditions, so the idea of Hell in Christian thought in particular is a distinctive one not found elsewhere. In addition, just as the way the Devil is thought of and represented changes over time, so the concept of Hell and the imagery associated with it has changed at various times in the past. In particular it altered dramatically during the later Renaissance. Today, the idea of Hell has lost much of its power for most people and has not shown the same kind of staying power as the Devil has. However, elements of the idea have migrated into popular culture and the basic idea may well make a comeback.

The Christian idea of Hell, like that of the Devil, emerged in the later part of antiquity. It combines two different ways of thinking about life after death that can be found in almost all of the world's religious traditions but the combination of the two is only found in Christianity and (to some degree) in Islam. Humans have apparently always speculated about what happens after death. An almost universal belief is that the self or person does not stop existing at death but persists in some form or other after death. This obviously poses the question of what kind of existence there is after death and whether it can be described or captured in physical terms. The result is that all over the world there is an elaborate mythology of the fate of the dead, their experience, and the place where they exist, the Underworld or afterlife. Interestingly these accounts are often extremely detailed and precise. However, despite their variety in some ways they share a number of common features and can be grouped into two broad types.

The commonest type of account of the afterlife and the Underworld is the kind found in Greek mythology, but also in many other mythological systems. In this almost everyone who dies goes to the same place. This is a location or state of existence associated with darkness and lack of any real capacity for action. It is thought of as being located underground, below the surface of the earth. Caves and underground rivers are often thought of as entrances to the Underworld or as marking its boundary. Everyone goes there regardless of the kind of life they have lived. In addition, for the overwhelming majority, there is neither punishment nor happiness. Instead the dead lead a rather dreary and dull existence, without feelings either positive or negative and with no real ability to interact with the world of the living or to actually do anything. They are seen as being like the shadow or memory of the actual living person, hence the common use of terms like 'shade' to describe them. Crucially, their existence is endless, eternal with no notion of return or rebirth. In this view the world of the deceased is essentially an enlarged and generalised version of the grave.

The world of the dead, the Underworld, is presided over in these accounts by a dark god or goddess who is harsh, stern, and implacable but also fair and just. The dark deity is a fearful and forbidding figure but is not malevolent and is part of the divine and natural order rather than an adversary. In its earliest forms it seems that the fate described above was shared by all, indiscriminately. However in traditions such as those of the Greeks and Romans but also others the idea arose that while the great majority would experience the kind of endless but neutral existence described, the exceptionally good and bad would receive special treatment although within the same place or world as the majority – they would be set aside in a special section or part of the Underworld as a whole. People who had been exceptionally wicked or had committed particularly egregious crimes or had angered the Gods would receive special (and often individually tailored) punishment while heroes and people of extraordinary wisdom or sanctity would enjoy a happy and pleasurable existence (although still a rather bland one by Christian standards). It is important to realise however that these two categories were a very small part of the dead in general.

This kind of afterlife and Underworld is found in most of the traditional polytheistic traditions. In classical mythology Hades rules over the subterranean underworld where most of the dead wander listlessly in the fields of Asphodel while a select few are punished in Tartarus or enjoy felicity in the Elysian Fields. For the Sumerians and Babylonians, the underworld of Kur or

Irallu was presided over by the grim goddess Erishkigal and her consort Nergal, the god of death, with the dead leading a listless and faded version of everyday life, consuming dust. In pagan Germanic myths those who died a heroic death went to eternal feasting and fighting in Valhalla while the great majority went to the foggy and cold realm of Niffelheim, governed by the goddess Hel who punished the particularly wicked in Hellheimr. We have a similar kind of picture in Japan (Yomi), Celtic mythology (Annwn in Wales and Tech Duinn in Ireland), Aztec and Mayan religion (Mictlan), and Finnish paganism (Tuonela). It is also a feature of traditional Jewish thought, with most of the dead going below the Earth to Sheol (literally 'dark') while a few are punished in Gehenna.

The other type of vision of the afterlife and the realm of the dead is found mainly in traditions that have reincarnation as a major feature, such as Hinduism, Buddhism, and Taoism. Here there are elaborate and complex realms of the dead that feature savage and intense punishment and suffering. This reflects the wrongs done by the deceased person during their lifetime. Crucially though, the punishment is purgative or cleansing and consequently is not eternal – it may last for a very long time but eventually the person will be reborn and return to the land of the living. This is what we find in Diyu (the Chinese hell), divided into ten 'courts' each presided over by a king and with its own particular kind of suffering and punishment. In Hindu thought there is Naraka, ruled by Yama, the god of Death and judge of the dead who rules over up to twenty-eight hells, each again having its own specific kind of torture to reflect the kinds of evil deeds being punished. The same pattern is found in Buddhism and Jainism.

So, most of the world's traditions have two views of the Underworld and afterlife: in one the existence of the dead is eternal but for the great majority dreary rather than particularly painful, in the other it is a place of intense suffering and punishment that is however not eternal but time limited and purgative. Both conceptions have the idea that the dead are judged but this is much more pronounced in the second one because of the need to determine the type and duration of punishment for each soul – in the first kind it is simply a matter of identifying the minority who receive exceptionally harsh or benign treatment. In both traditions the realm or dimension of the dead is ruled by a figure who is grim and fearsome (literally dreadful) but not evil or malevolent.

Just as with the idea of the Devil, it was the old Persian religion of Zoroastrianism that began a transformation of the concept of the afterlife and Hell. What happened had the following elements. Firstly, the idea of testing or judgment was made a central part of the story. This was captured in the dramatic image of the Chinvat bridge, which all souls had to cross after death: for the virtuous it was wide and easy, for the wicked narrow and difficult. The virtuous passed over to a happy state while the wicked plunged off the bridge into a place of suffering and punishment. The critical innovation was that the condition of punishment would last for as long as the physical universe endured, so the souls of the damned would not be released through rebirth. In this way a new conception of the afterlife arose, one that combined the eternity of the first with the elaborate punishments of the second.

The idea created by Zoroastrians also incorporated another element of many older notions but elaborated it. While the commonest conceptions of the Underworld did not see it as a place of punishment for the majority or the seat of an evil power, there was a frequently occurring belief that some of its inhabitants, or staff as we might say, were harmful and hostile spiritual powers or demons. Thus the ancient Mesopotamians believed that the underworld of Arallu was inhabited by demons such as Pazuzu, the personification of the winds that brought disease and plagues of locusts, while for the Greeks Tartarus was the home of the Furies, tasked by the gods with persecuting and punishing those who had provoked them or broken particularly significant moral rules. In the Zoroastrian conception, hell or Duzakh was associated with Ahriman, the evil god, and with his servants the Daevas so Hell become a distinct afterlife, separate from the one experienced by the virtuous and inhabited and ruled over by malevolent spiritual beings.

As with the demonic, this set of ideas came to influence Judaism in particular. During the period of messianic or apocalyptic Judaism (between roughly the Maccabean Revolt and the second century AD) the idea that there was an afterlife consisting of punishment for the wicked took root and became combined with the idea of the apocalypse, the dramatic end of the world and time when God's purpose and plan would be revealed (the term apocalypse literally means 'unveiling'). The belief that took shape was that after death some were rewarded and others punished until the final judgement. At that point of final judgment, the virtuous would go to live forever with God. The final fate of the wicked had two versions. In one they would be annihilated and cease to exist – a 'second death'. In the other they would be condemned to an eternal fate in a place of punishment, along with evil spiritual powers.

These are the ideas that we find in the Gospels and early Christian writings. They are particularly prominent in *Matthew's Gospel*, where the various parables found in *Mark* and *Luke* have additional endings that describe how those who are not saved or do not receive the good news will be cast into fire or the place of wailing and gnashing of teeth. Typically, this is something that will take place at the end of time and the final judgment. However, one particular parable, in *St Luke's Gospel*, firmly fixed two ideas in early Christian thinking. The first was that the state of punishment began after death, even if it was then confirmed at the final judgment. The second was that Hell was a physical place, like the traditional underworld, and with physical punishment and pain. This was of course the story of Dives and Lazarus, which also clearly made punishment the result not only of rejecting the gospel but also of failure to follow the demands of virtue (in this case charity).

At the same time that the Christian idea of the Devil took firm shape, so did that of Hell – in fact it makes sense to think of the two things as aspects of the same intellectual process. Much of this can be traced in the multitudinous apocalyptic writings that were produced between the second and fifth centuries. These often contained detailed accounts of the sufferings and punishment of the damned after the apocalypse and the end of days. The accounts show an extraordinary degree of vindictiveness and resentment against people seen to have violated moral rules or persecuted Jews and Christians and a particular obsession with the punishment of those who had violated sexual norms (for example in the *Apocalypse of Peter*). At the same time Hell was integrated into the narrative of the Devil and his deeds that was being put together at that time.

In this story Hell was the place that the Devil and his fellow rebel angels went to after their expulsion from Heaven following the failure of their rebellion. At this time they could still move freely around the world because following the Fall they were in control of it, the Devil being the ruler of this world. Because of the Fall, all human beings born subsequently were in the Devil's hands and subject to him. This meant that on death they would go to Hell, a kind of vast prison for them that was also the seat of the Devil's power and his stronghold. After his death on the Cross, according to the Apostles' Creed, Jesus having died, descended into Hell. What then took place was what in Christian legend became known as the Harrowing of Hell in which Christ defeated Satan and bound him, and preached the gospel to all of those confined in Hell. He then freed a multitude of them, including the Patriarchs and other figures from the Old Testament, who were then led to Heaven. After spending three days in Hell he departed and rose from the dead in the Resurrection. The Devil is now bound in Hell and imprisoned there but he will be released in the end times, as described in the book of Revelations. At that point the final battle and the apocalypse will take place and the last judgment. Following this he and his servants will be cast into the lake of fire (identified with Hell) and either destroyed or bound there for eternity.

This narrative led to a number of subsequent ideas that tidied it up or softened the harshness of the simple message. One was the idea of limbo, meaning a condition in which a person was separated from God and therefore unable to enjoy the beatific vision (the direct experience of God) but not experiencing pain or suffering. In fact, by some accounts souls in Limbo experience the highest possible degree of natural felicity and happiness, they are only denied the ultimate (and unimaginable) pleasure of direct communion with God. This idea was initially used to explain the fate of people such as the heroes and Patriarchs of the Old Testament who according to the account had gone to Hell until the Harrowing. It seemed rather harsh that they should suffer the same fate as the wicked and so the idea came of Limbo, a part of Hell but not a place of suffering, where they were held until Christ came. The idea of Limbo was later extended to include two other categories. The first was unbaptised infants, given the argument of Saint Augustine that the act of generation being sinful after the fall meant that all people born were marked by sin as a result rather than being born immaculate (this is what is meant by 'original sin' – the Orthodox Churches do not accept this, nor do Jews or Muslims). Since a child that dies in infancy before baptism has not committed any sinful acts the conclusion was that they also were in Limbo. The second were virtuous pagans who lived before the incarnation and therefore had no opportunity for salvation. For some authors such as Dante they were also in Limbo (as well as others, since he places Saladin there in his Divine Comedy). For other authors they would be in Limbo until the coming of Jesus into Hell but would then accept the Gospel like the Patriarchs. Much later (in the twelfth century) there is the development of the idea of Purgatory, an intermediate state between Heaven and Hell where the souls of the saved dead are purged of sin for a long but finite period of time before being admitted to heaven – an idea that owes much to older pagan and Jewish ideas. It proved to be a useful money raising device for the Catholic Church but this came to backfire on them since it was the initial source of Luther's protests and subsequently the Reformation.

So, by the end of antiquity the main ideas of Hell had been formulated and combined with or folded into the narrative of the Devil. The predominant Christian notion of Hell combined the typical polytheistic idea of an everlasting state of affairs with the Hindu or Buddhist one of a condition of punishment, so the key belief is that for all who reject the offer of salvation posed by the Gospel there will be an eternal punishment. This combination as the default state of the great majority of the dead is distinctive since as explained earlier the two predominant traditions before then were of an eternal afterlife that was not particularly painful for the great majority or an intensely painful one that was time limited. However, there was disagreement over exactly how things would work out eventually. Everyone apart from the minority who adopted the position of mortalism (which is that the dead do not continue to have consciousness and will 'rest' until they are revived at the last judgment) thought that the wicked and those who had rejected salvation would go to Hell. The disagreement was over what would happen at the end of time after the last judgment. One view, annihilationism, held that the wicked would be destroyed, they would experience a second and final death. The other was that they, along with the living found wanting at the final judgment, would be condemned to eternal punishment. This was the majority view in earlier times, mainly because of the great influence of Saint Augustine.

The other central aspect of the doctrine of Hell as it emerged was that it was not only real (in the philosophical sense of existing – not everything that exists is physical) but also an actual physical place and that the fires of hell were similarly physical. This meant that the pains inflicted on the damned were also physical and, beyond the worst that the human mind could conceive. This was in addition to the spiritual and psychological anguish and despair of being utterly cut off from God and rejected by him. A critical aspect of this is that the condition of the inhabitants of Hell is totally hopeless, there is no possibility of their release or of an end to or mitigation of their punishment (thus rejecting the heresy of universalism, according to which in time all humans at least will be saved). Modern theology has tended to reject this severe vision but for centuries it was the predominant one, particularly among Western Christians.

The Islamic idea of Hell, which took shape during the early years of that faith under the Umayyad and the early Abbasid Caliphs, also incorporated ideas from Jewish apocalypticism as well as deriving mainly from the many passages in the Quran that deal with the afterlife and the fate of unbelievers and the wicked. Jahannum as it is called (a name related to the Hebrew Gehenna), is very similar to the Christian conception of hell, being a place of fire, boiling water, and extreme cold and many torments and punishments for the wicked and those who do not follow the true religion (particularly idolaters). The overwhelming consensus of Islamic scholars is that most people do not exist as conscious entities after death but exist in a state of suspended animation until the final judgment after which the wicked will be confined to Jahannum and the virtuous believers will ascend to paradise or Jannah (meaning 'garden'). Like Zoroastrians, the belief is that at judgment all will pass over a bridge (As-Sirat) with the wicked and unbelievers falling off it to plunge into Hell. There is no consensus among scholars as to the duration of Hell with some seeing it as temporary (so more like Purgatory) while others see it as eternal.

While the nature of Hell and its relation to the story of Satan and his doings were established by the end of antiquity, the details of Hell, what we may call its geography, were worked out during the Middle Ages. This took place in both Christianity and Islam. This period also saw the establishing of a definite iconography, which remains so much a part of the Western mind that it can be immediately recognised by almost anyone from that tradition even today (in contrast to the way that Hindu or Buddhist iconography for example will not be). Interestingly the iconography of Hell in Christianity and Islam is sufficiently similar that someone from either tradition can recognise it and make sense of it, despite differences. This reveals the extent to which the two faiths are related, and closer to each other than either is to other and older traditions such as Hinduism, Buddhism, or Taoism. In Islam the working out was done principally through exegesis by scholars of the Quran and the Hadith (traditions or stories of episodes in the life of the Prophet) while in Christianity it took the form mainly of accounts of visions of Hell and the afterlife, known as vision literature, and related to the genre of 'fantastic voyages'.

The best known and most influential medieval vision narrative was the *Vision of Tundal*, written in Ireland in the twelfth century. It was amazingly popular and was translated into at least fifteen languages as early as the fifteenth century. The narrator Tundal is supposedly an Irish knight who has led a carnal and dissolute life. While ill he falls into a coma for three days. During that time, he has a vision in which he visits Hell and experiences some of the torments it contains. He is among other torments chewed and torn apart by demons who castrate him, eaten by a bird with a steel beak that then excretes him as a snake into a freezing lake, tortured by extreme heat and cold, melted in a furnace and combined with other sinners, and attacked by savage beasts. He sees damned souls suspended on hooks through their intestines over red hot coals, begging for mercy as they melt and burn. Eventually at the bottom of Hell he sees the Devil, a monstrous creature with thousands of hands with razor sharp nails who breathes in and swallows the souls of the dead like smoke before defecating them onto hot coals, while grasping thousands of others and tearing them apart. The ultimate horror is that there is no release in death, as the mangled damned are constantly restored so that new punishments can be visited on them. Faced with this, when he wakes up Tundal repents his sins and becomes a monk.

Tundal's *Vision* was only one of many published in the Middle Ages, although the content of all of them was very similar. They reveal both a vivid imagination and an extraordinary vicarious sadism along with an obsessive interest in sexual transgressions in particular. The picture that emerges is very distinct and recognisable. Hell is a place of intense and unbearable heat, stinking smoke, and sulphurous winds. It is also a place of extreme and agonising cold. It is the location for ingeniously imagined and carefully described tortures of all kinds, with the damned being boiled, burned, stabbed, sliced and impaled, flayed, and disembowelled. A common image is that of the dead being repeatedly devoured and eaten before being excreted entire for the process to continue. Hell is not uniform, but divided into different areas or territories, each with its own particular horrors and punishments. It is dark and without light and yet its inhabitants and visitors can see, which adds to their horror and anguish. All of the senses are assaulted as Hell is a place of vile stench and terrible cacophonous noise produced by the screams and sobbing of the damned. The landscape is one of desolation and waste, with countless pits and crevasses. There are rivers but they are rivers of fire, or boiling blood, poison, or sharp knives. The entrance to Hell is most often the gaping mouth of a vast beast or monster and the Mouth of Hell was a favourite topic in iconography. Sometimes Hell itself is actually a colossal monster, with the landscapes and torments located inside it. The size of Hell is indeterminate but enormous. This raised the problem of where it was, if it was indeed a physical place. One solution was to make it the interior of the Earth but sometimes it was described as being so large that even that was not enough and it became a parallel and physical world (employing the medieval doctrine of the plurality of worlds).

In Islam the physical punishments are very similar but Jahannum is more organised than Hell was at that time. It is divided into seven levels, each with its own entrance or gate. Each level is for a different kind or category of sinner, with the deeper levels reserved for the most heinous and punishments becoming more severe as you go down. Conventionally the first three levels are for Muslims, Christians, and Jews (in that order) and are temporary, purgative hells. The very bottom is reserved for Iblis and other rebellious spiritual beings, and hypocrites, those who in life claimed to be believers but were not – the worst of all sinners and the most hateful to God according to the Prophet and the scholars. Above Jahannum is the As-Sirat bridge, as narrow as a hair and as sharp as a razor while at the bottom and centre is the tree Zakkum, monstrous and twisted and growing out of fire, that bears poisonous fruit in the shape of demons heads, which the damned have to eat and which explode within them and tear their bodies apart.

Medieval vision literature culminates in and is concluded and replaced by the work of Dante. In the first part of his great work the *Divine Comedy*, Dante is taken on a guided tour of Hell by the Roman poet Vergil (here representing human reason). This has similarities with the vision literature in terms of the content but is couched differently. Instead of being presented as a vision it is described as being an actual journey (metaphorically representing the journey of the soul through life and from a lost state to salvation) and so it is closer to the genre of the fantastic voyage that was popular in both the earlier Middle Ages and after Dante's time in the Renaissance and Baroque periods. Dante's Hell, like the Islamic one, is organised and structured. It is a vast conical pit, under the Northern Hemisphere with its epicentre under Jerusalem, and extending down to the very centre of the Earth. It consists of nine successive concentric circles, each devoted to a particular sin and its associated punishment, with the gravity of the sin increasing as you descend further into the pit. The nine circles are divided into three groups, reflecting Dante's adopting the Aristotelian division of sin and vice as being of three kinds: sins of incontinence reflecting inability to control the appetites, sins of violence, and sins of fraud and malice. (The degree of severity of sin is in the same order). Hell is entered via a huge gate with the motto over it that has passed from Dante into popular knowledge "Lay down all hope, all ye who enter here". Behind it is the antechamber, containing a huge crowd of people (Dante remarks *"I had not thought, Death had undone so many"*) who refused to choose between good and evil and are condemned to rush aimlessly to and fro for eternity. The first circle is Limbo, where the virtuous pagans reside. Beyond there is Hell proper in the shape of circles two to nine with in order the lustful, the gluttonous, the prodigal and avaricious, the wrathful, heretics, the violent, the fraudulent, and finally, traitors. Several of the circles are subdivided to allow for different types of the broader category.

Dante gives an account that, like earlier ones, emphasises the physical nature of Hell and its punishments. His genius as a poet means that these descriptions are varied and vivid. He also captures the physical conditions, the cacophonous noise, the stench, and the alternation of heat and cold. There are many vivid images such as that of the wood of suicides in the circle of the violent, where those who took their own lives are transformed into twisted and tormented trees, suffering in silence as birds tear at their leaves. There are also detailed descriptions of the torments and punishments but unlike in the vision literature the emphasis is not so much upon the physical suffering (although there is plenty of that) but rather on kinds of punishment that either reflect the sin or contrast with it (this enables Dante to explore exactly what the nature of each sin is and exactly why it alienates the sinner from God). So, for example fortune tellers are condemned to walk with their heads twisted backwards, unable to see where they are going. (No doubt an updated version would have that section populated by economic and political forecasters). At the very bottom of hell are three categories of traitors and betrayers, frozen in ice. The Devil is in the middle of them as the greatest of betrayers, at the base and centre of Hell. The description of Satan (for more detail of which see chapter 10) makes it clear that Hell is mainly a vast prison and place of punishment, for the damned and above all for the defeated Enemy.

During the Renaissance, just as the Devil underwent a transformation, so did Hell. The older idea of a physical Hell certainly persisted, particularly among the general population However, among the educated in all denominations there was a clear shift. There was more emphasis on Hell's being a state of separation from God, and increasingly the focus was on the psychological state and condition of its inmates rather than their physical state. The conclusion of this was for Hell to become a state of mind rather than a particular physical place. This meant that people could be in Hell while apparently still in the everyday physical world. The classic early expression of this was in Christopher Marlowe's play *Doctor Faustus*. In this adaptation of the Faust legend Marlowe describes how the prideful and egocentric Faust summons the demon Mephistopheles in order to gain unlimited knowledge and power in return for selling his soul. He asks Mephistopheles what he is and is told he is one of the fallen angels who rebelled with Lucifer and now is in Hell with Lucifer. Faust then asks how he can be out of Hell and with Faust to which Mephistopheles replies *"Why this is Hell, nor am I out of it. Thinkst thou that I, who saw the face of God and tasted the eternal joy of Heaven, am not tormented with ten thousand hells in being deprived of everlasting bliss?"* Later in another conversation Mephistopheles says *"Within the bowels of these elements, Where we are tortured, and remain for ever. Hell hath no limits, nor is circumscribed In one self place; but where we are is hell, And where hell is, there must we ever be. And to be short, when all the world dissolves, And every creature shall be purified, All places shall be hell that is not heaven"*.

In other words, Marlowe is saying that Hell is not a physical place with a particular location, it is rather a state of mind and so can be wherever the person who is in that state happens to be. Its essence is the knowledge of being utterly and hopelessly separated from

God, and the despair and self-hatred that comes with that. The only response that damned spirits such as Mephistopheles have is to feed their malice and self-hatred by seeking to subvert others so that they come to their share their fate, in an act of monumental spite. This emphasis is also found in Paradise Lost, when Satan declares *"The mind is its own place, and in itself can make a Heaven of Hell, a Hell of Heaven"* which makes both Heaven and Hell a matter of radical subjectivism. Marlowe also hints at another idea, that this world that we live in is actually Hell, although for us there is a chance of escape, unlike the damned Mephistopheles or the hapless Faust. These understandings of Hell and what it is have become ever more dominant in the modern world and in the more recent past and present it is the second one that has become widespread, although the first is still very powerful.

In the later eighteenth and nineteenth century onwards Hell and its traditional iconography has been used as a way of describing and critiquing the industrial city and the social world it has created. This can be seen first in William Blake's reference in *Jerusalem* to 'dark, satanic mills' but there are other examples, such as T. S. Eliot in *The Wasteland* using the phrase from Dante quoted earlier as the narrator looks at the crowds pouring over Westminster Bridge. Artists such as John Martin combined traditional depictions of Hell with images drawn from the contemporary city, so partly criticising the latter. (For a deeper account of the portrayal of Hell and the Devil in representational art see Chapter 10 below).

The view of many observers though is that in the modern world the old idea of Hell as a physical place that we find in Dante and Tundal has decisively lost its hold on the popular mind. This was the point made by George Orwell when he remarked that even those who said they believed in Hell no longer believed in it in the way they believed in the existence of Australia. The fact that people hardly thought about Hell, or regarded it as a matter of fun and humour, showed that they did not take it seriously. Orwell himself thought this was inevitable and even in some ways desirable but also alarming and disturbing because it had removed one of the foundations of most people's sense of morality.

However, the idea of Hell as a state of mind retains its power. Increasingly also, with the horrors that totalitarianism and modern war have brought, the idea of Hell has come to be used as a way of capturing the kinds of physical experience that have existed in places such as the Western Front, the death camps of the Holocaust, the Gulag and Laogai, or in cities under aerial bombardment or during genocides such as the Holocaust, Cambodia, Rwanda, and Armenia. The traditional idea of Hell as a place and experience of intense suffering, degradation and despair that is brought about by the working of a kind of pure malice, cruelty, and evil that cannot be reduced to simple ideology or self-interest is the most powerful tool we have for understanding these kinds of phenomena and experience. In addition the hopelessness and feeling of abandonment and futility that so many feel when experiencing or even reading or thinking about such things can be captured in the idea that the essence of Hell is the abandoning of belief in God or virtue and the feeling of loss and separation from all that is good and true that follows. In this way Hell is seen as still having a physical reality, in the events and conditions as well as the psychological states, that are brought about by certain features of the modern world, including the attenuation of faith that a succession of authors from Matthew Arnold on Dover Beach to George Orwell have noted.

In much popular culture Hell is treated humorously and light heartedly, as for example in South Park. There also too many films to mention where the execrable quality reveals not only low budgets and poor direction but an inability to grasp the real meaning of the concept. However, there are other works such as the film *Tales From the Hood*, which sees the life of inner city African Americans as being in some sense living in Hell. The idea of Hell as either place and condition or state of mind retains much power, because it is so closely connected to the undoubtedly real phenomena of pain, suffering and apparently motiveless evil.

Further Reading
Bruce, Scott G. (ed.) (2019) *The Penguin Book of Hell*. Penguin.

Bernstein, Alan E. (1996) *The Formation of Hell: Death and Retribution in the Ancient and Early Christian Worlds*. Cornell University Press.

Bernstein, Alan E. (2017) *Hell and Its Rivals: Death and Retribution Among Christians, Jews, and Muslims in the Early Middle Ages*. Cornell University Press.

Casey, John (2010) *After Lives: A Guide to Heaven, Hell, and Purgatory*. Oxford University Press.

Ehrman, Bart D. (2020) *Heaven and Hell: A History of the Afterlife*. Oneworld Publications.

Gardiner, Eileen (2008) *Visions of Heaven and Hell Before Dante*. Italica Press.

Gray, Alasdair (2018) *Hell: Dante's Divine Trilogy Part One*. Canongate Books.

Kastan, David Scott (ed.) (2005) *Marlowe: Doctor Faustus*. Norton Critical Editions.

Kirkpatrick, Robin (trans. & ed.) (2006) *Dante: Inferno*. Penguin.

Kogon, Eugene (2006 1st published 1980) *The Theory and Practice of Hell: The German Concentration Camps and the System Behind Them*. Macmillan USA.

Turner, Alice K. (1993). *The History of Hell*. Harcourt Brace.

Van Scott, Miriam (1998). *Encyclopedia of Hell*. St Martin's Press.

http://www.hell-on-line.org/index.html

https://www.artsy.net/article/artsy-editorial-11-nightmarish-depictions-hell-art-history

http://www.worldofdante.org/gallery_dore.html (a good introduction to Gustave Dore's illustrations of Dante's Inferno).

Chapter 7. The Devil's Allies: Demons, Demonology, and Creatures of the Dark

One of the main features of the idea of the Devil is that he is not alone. He is not a unique creature, with nothing else like him in the universe. Rather he is one of a kind or type of being or entity, the most powerful to be sure, but not the only one. He is not a solitary creature, isolated and alone but is a member or part of a kind of society of creatures like himself who interact with each other, sometimes competing but more often cooperating. Above all he is not a lone operator, he does not do things on his own, he has many willing and equally malign collaborators. These all share his essential nature: like him they are spiritual beings that have rebelled against God and been eternally damned as a result, motivated by pure malevolence to do ill and seek to thwart or pervert the will of God. This wider category is that of the demonic and the working out of the details of this set of ideas was a crucial part of the development of the story and concept of Satan. The process gave rise to an entire discipline or area of study, that of demonology, which continues to this day.

Human beings in all times and places before the modern have believed in the existence of invisible and immaterial beings that despite that lack of physicality can have visible and perceptible effects on the material world. Frequently they are thought to be non-material but able to manifest as physical under certain circumstances or to be able to indicate or reveal their presence and actions by physical and visible signs. It is only in the modern world and not everywhere then that this belief in a world full of spirits and haunted and moved by them, has waned. Alongside the world of spiritual entities most societies have also believed in the existence of physical yet supernatural or uncanny creatures and entities, including many that are intelligent and people in a sense, while not being human. What both classes of being share is the quality of being magical, of not being bound by the physical rules and limits that constrain the merely human.

It is hard for people born in much of the modern world to realise just how pervasive and important these beliefs were for our ancestors. Since the later eighteenth century, they have been put into the capacious category of superstition and contrasted with formal knowledge and explanations, particularly scientific ones, but before then they were a part of the mental furniture of all kinds of people including the educated. In every age and society, they were a crucial way of explaining events and happenings in the world. This meant both good and beneficial events and ones that were damaging and harmful. Anything for which there was not an obvious and direct physical cause – and a fair number even of those – were accounted for as the result of the actions of spiritual and magical beings. Our ancestors lived in what the late Carl Sagan called a demon-haunted world.

That expression though comes with a weight of meaning for those with a Christian heritage that it does not have for somebody from a different civilisational inheritance, even that of Judaism or Islam. The magical and spiritual beings that humans have historically believed in were part of the natural order. Some were friendly and were associated with good fortune and beneficial happenings, such as good health, prosperity, love and sexual pleasure (and the consequence, children), security, and longevity. Others were hostile and dangerous, associated with bad fortune and things such as illness, hunger and its causes such as drought or things that caused crops to fail and livestock to die, personal misfortune and death. In particular harmful or dangerous spirits were associated with deranged or irrational behaviour and states of mind, what we would now call mental illness. This was explained instead as the result of the actions of hostile spirits or magical entities, through the mechanism of possession, an idea found in almost every culture. This was actually a convincing way of explaining many of the features of mental illnesses such as schizophrenia, such as hearing voices. Such hostile and dangerous spiritual powers and entities were feared and hated but they were thought of as the representatives of the dark side of the cosmos, hostile to humans and their interests in the way that pests and vermin were. The idea of the demonic and of demons as a kind of malevolent entity (as opposed to merely hostile or dangerous) is a feature of Christian thinking in particular, one that became part of the story of the Devil.

The actual term demon is a Greek one (originally daimon) and referred to a particular class of spiritual being. A daimon was a kind of personal guardian spirit associated with or attached to a specific individual (an idea recently revived by the author Philip

Pullman). Socrates famously declared that he had one for example. A daimon would give advice and put ideas into the mind of the person to whom it was attached. This Greek idea was also found in other cultures and passed from the Greeks into subsequent ones, such as Islam. There it took the form of a folk belief that everyone had two invisible beings sat on their shoulders and whispering suggestions into their ears: the right hand one urged virtuous acts, the one on the left sinful ones – an idea also found in Tom and Jerry cartoons! The Hellenistic world (the period between the death of Alexander and the rise of Rome) was one where this kind of idea was commonplace. As well as personal spirits, there were spiritual beings associated with natural phenomena such as trees and springs or rivers (the dryads and naiads), weather, and places or locations (the genius loci of the Romans). All households had spirits associated with them that were regarded as minor deities and venerated as the household gods (the lares and penates of Roman households).

As this last showed, the dividing line between spirits and gods was a blurred and indeterminate one – in a very real sense the gods and goddesses were creatures of the same kind as minor spirits and household gods but with more powers and responsibilities. Alongside the invisible and intangible beings such as the daimons were supernatural entities thought of as very much physical such as fauns and satyrs and all of the other creatures of Greek mythology. The ancient Israelites were a part of this world and shared many of its beliefs. However, in the period after the Babylonian captivity their monotheism became much firmer with the critical transition from being followers of a god who was one among many (even if 'jealous' i.e. possessive and not prepared to share worship) to believing that their god (Yahweh or Jehovah) was the one and only God. This meant that during the Second Temple period Jewish thought developed a set of distinctive views about spiritual beings, which then passed in amended form into Christianity and helped to form the notion of the demonic and of demons as a very particular kind of spiritual power.

In Jewish thought at this time spiritual beings were mainly part of the world that God had created. Some though had either been among the very first things created or had existed before the physical world was brought into existence. The most important of these were angels. The term 'angel' is derived from the Greek word *'angelos'* which means a messenger. This was used at a later date as the translation for a variety of words used in the Hebrew Old Testament texts to refer to spiritual beings who were agents or emissaries of God, directly dependent upon him and agents and executors of his will. The commonest though is *malakh* which also means 'messenger'. They appear frequently in the various books of the Old Testament, sometimes with names (as in the Apocryphal book *Tobit* where Raphael appears) but more often unnamed. The *Book of Enoch* in particular went into great detail about angels, their power, and the part they played as the direct executors of the divine will, who gave it effect. As explained earlier, that apocryphal work also introduced the idea that some of these angels had rebelled (the Watchers) through lusting after human women and had become rebels from god and banished to this world. The Jewish scriptures also came to define the gods of the people of the Levant such as Baal, Ashtaroth (actually Astarte, the Levantine goddess of love), Moloch, and Berith as being also hostile spiritual powers and enemies of the true God: their existence was accepted, as was their spiritual nature, but they were denied divinity or to be worthy of worship as that was reserved for God.

As explained earlier, all of this became a crucial part of the concept and story of the Devil. He became a rebel angel, like the Watchers but with a different narrative attached to him, having rebelled against God before the creation of the physical world and being cast out of heaven before gaining vengeance upon God (as he thought) by bringing about the Fall of Adam and Eve. Angels appear frequently in the New Testament at various points, bringing succour and relief to Jesus himself and to the Apostles at various points. There are also repeated references to demons, and casting out demons from people possessed by them was one of the most frequent miracles performed by Jesus and, after his death and resurrection, the disciples. At this point demons of this kind are the hostile and dangerous spirit beings found in all of the world's various cultures and casting out spirits of this kind was a regular function of holy men and prophets. The crucial step was to combine this belief with the idea of an angelic rebellion.

In this Lucifer had not rebelled on his own. Instead, he had subverted many of his fellow angels who had joined him in rebellion. The usual figure as a proportion of all angels was one third. This derived from a passage in Revelations where we are told that the Dragon (identified as the Devil) had brought down a third of the stars of heaven. This text was understood as meaning that a third of the angelic hosts (identified with the stars) had shared his rebellion and fall. This made sense because the name Lucifer, now firmly attached to the Devil and used in Isaiah in the passage that was the foundation of the notion that he was a rebel angel, referred to the morning star (the planet Venus – the word lucifer means light bringer) so if he was a star the other stars that he brought down must be angels as well. The term demon was now used as the label for his fellow rebel angels. What Christian thinking did was to extend the category of demon to include all of the spiritual beings and powers of the old pagan religions. Thus, all of the nature spirits and magical beings of folklore became fallen spirits, banished to earth for their rebellion.

During the Middle Ages this was elaborated. A distinction was drawn between those fallen beings who were originally of higher status or whose rebellion and support of Satan had been more egregious, and the other ones, of lesser power and (perhaps) degree of blame. The former were demons proper, who had fallen into Hell with the Devil and were thought of as being entities like him, former angels who had rebelled. The various pagan deities were thought by the Church to be in this category – they were rebel angels who had deceived and deluded people into worshipping them and following their teachings. Things like fairies or nature spirit were lesser beings whose fall had not been so marked: instead of falling all the way into Hell they had been cast into the physical world, to plague and harass humans. Beings like fairies were therefore always dangerous and malevolent in the eyes of the Church and believers were not supposed to have converse with them. In practice the Church found it difficult to enforce this, because the belief in magical beings living alongside human society was so powerful, long-established, and pervasive that it was impossible to root out. In practice the Church would tolerate folk rituals and beliefs even while officially disapproving of them. After the Reformation the Protestant denominations were much more hostile and made sustained efforts to stamp out such folk beliefs but again found this difficult. There was no compromise where the more powerful and dangerous fallen spirits were concerned however – these were the enemies of all that was good and having anything to do with them was to court damnation.

There was a similar theory in Islamic thinking. There the belief was that Allah had created many beings as well as human beings and the creatures of the animal kingdom. Among these were djinn.

There were entities of great power, composed of the element of fire (and so elementals of a sort). They were not universally malevolent, so that aspect of Christian thinking was absent. The Devil, Iblis, was originally one and he had many followers who aided him in his work of tempting people and obstructing the pursuit of virtue. Usually known as ifrit, these corresponded to the demons of Christian thinking but the important difference was that djinni as a class were not inherently evil. They were also thought of as being on a par with human beings because they shared the same status as them relative to Allah. Also, although undetectable by the senses for most of the time, they were not thought to be immaterial or spiritual beings.

The kind of detailed accounts of demons found in Christian demonology (see below) are not a feature of Islamic thought although ill-disposed djinni or shaitans (closer to the Christian idea of a demon) feature prominently in Islamic folklore and mythology. Jewish thought and folklore have many spiritual or supernatural entities that resemble the Christian demons but again they are not part of an elaborate and detailed picture of the cosmos. The original widespread idea was that of the shedim, dangerous and harmful nature spirits that caused illnesses and natural disasters. There were also other entities such as the dybbuk, the soul or ghost of a deceased person that possessed the living and used them and the *qlipoth* (literally husks or rinds) that were the evil counterparts of the sephiroth in kabbalistic thought. These though were not actual persons but rather principles, of obstruction and difficulty, that held back people from the divine.

The Jewish myth that went on to have the most influence on later Christian thought was that of Lilith. Originally this seems to have been a name for a type of night-spirit that abducted or killed young children, although the word is often translated as screech-owl. In later Jewish legend and commentary she was the first wife of Adam, created at the same time as him. The relevant text is *Genesis 1:27* "*So God created man in his own image, in the image of God created he him; male and female created he them.*" (The creation of Eve from a rib of Adam is later, in *Genesis 2:22*). The narrative of Lilith is first developed in a medieval apocryphal work, *The Alphabet of Ben-Sirach*. According to this Lilith and Adam did not get on because she insisted that she was equal to him and in particular refused to lie below him for sex (Adam for his part insisted that he went on top). After this she flew away to the sea and had sex with many demons, producing many demonic offspring as a result. Adam complained to God who sent angels after Lilith but she refused to return and the outcome was a deal by which she agreed to kill a hundred of her children every day. She came to be seen as a queen of demons and in later Jewish and Christian folklore was linked with the demon Asmodeus, who had appeared as the king of malign spirits in the apocryphal work Tobit. She has two distinct personae in later tales, firstly as a demon of female lust, a seductress, and secondly as a witch or evil power who brings about the death of new-born infants. The two kinds of portrayal or roles are almost never found together. In later occult thinking she becomes the preeminent female demon, even the spouse or lover of the Devil himself.

In medieval Christianity the idea of the demons as fallen angels was much elaborated. A crucial notion was that, just like the Devil himself, the other fallen angels, the demons, were persons. That meant that although the number of them was very large, each one was a distinct creature with its own name, powers, qualities and attributes. A similar view was taken with regard to angels, where the largely indistinguishable angels of the Old testament were organised into a complex hierarchy of types and degrees of angelic power, with many given particular names and attributes. The work that began this was a fifth century book called *The Celestial Hierarchy*. We do not know the name of the author or indeed anything much about him but he presented his works as being by Dionysus the Areopagite, one of the converts of St Paul who is mentioned in the *Acts*. Consequently, he is always referred to as the Pseudo-Dionysus. According to him, there were nine types or orders of angel, grouped into three choirs, ranked by their proximity to God. These were in order Seraphim, Cherubim, and Thrones; Dominations, Virtues, and Powers; Principalities, Archangels, and Angels. Each order of angels had their particular powers and functions in the cosmic order. All this generated the whole discipline of angelology, the branch of theology concerned with the nature and function of angels.

Since demons were fallen angels and retained much of their angelic nature, albeit perverted and corrupted, it followed that they were also organised in a hierarchy, except that this was an infernal one rather than heavenly. Just as there was a discipline of angelology, so there was a corresponding one of demonology. This was worked out during the Middle Ages and enormously elaborated in detail during the Renaissance. Since demons were originally angels, they had the same qualities of nature. They were spiritual rather than material (but able to affect the material world), immortal, and immutable – that is their nature did not change and they had a perfect will, which meant that having rebelled they could never repent. Like angels they were of different kinds (depending on which type of angel they had once been) and each kind had its own powers, knowledge and qualities. Their number and the structure of the hierarchy was worked out in a number of books. The most influential of these was the *Pseudomonarchia Daemonum*, by the Dutch writer Johann Weyer. This was actually a part of a larger work by Weyer, the *De Praestigiis Daemonum* (*On the Trickery of Demons*), which he published in 1577. This was a sceptical work that criticised the then powerful belief in the existence and real powers of witches. Weyer thought that this was a delusion but one produced by the trickery of demons, who he firmly thought were real.

Weyer worked out, following earlier writers, that when Satan rebelled and fell, he took with him 666 legions of demons. Each legion contained 6,666 demons and the whole array was ruled by 66 major figures, making 4,439,622 in total. An earlier estimate was 133,316,666. Works of demonology produced at this time (the Renaissance) assigned names to the major figures in the infernal hierarchy and identified their previous angelic order and rank. This in turn determined what kinds of knowledge they had and the kinds of powers they could exercise. They were also given titles such as duke, marquess, count, earl and so forth, making Hell and the kingdom of the Devil a kind of replica of the Renaissance monarchies of the time, with major demons corresponding to the aristocracy. Some demons were also ministers, exercising governmental functions in the infernal kingdom (again on the lines of an actual monarchy of the time).

What also appeared at this time was the idea that, although treacherous, deceitful and dangerous, as well as powerful, these demonic lords could be controlled and used as servants of a kind by a sufficiently adept magician or wizard. This was the through discipline of goetia, the use of formal rituals and apparatus to evoke and call up and then bind and use demonic spiritual powers. The point was that many of these powers and the knowledge associated with them were useful for human beings – if only the demons in question could be got to cooperate. Despite the warnings of the Church many people were attracted by the idea and the result was the production of handbooks on how to do this, which contained rituals for evoking and binding demons and descriptions of them (so that they could be recognised) and of the things that they could do and the particular kinds of knowledge that they had.

So demonological treatises were broadly of two kinds. One type categorised and classified demons and set out their modes of operation (the kinds of particular sin they led people into) so that they could be guarded against – such works often assigned a saint to each demon, who would work against it. The other type were manuals for summoning demons, who are also categorised and ordered in the same way. These were the infamous grimoires or works of magical evocation. In these there are elaborate instructions on how to construct a summoning circle or diagram, often in the shape of a pentacle or five-pointed star in which the summoned demon will appear while being confined. As well as instructions as to the symbols that had to be written in and around the circle, there are also elaborate spells and rituals, invocations and chants that worked to evoke the demon and also bind it. The best known of these include *The Sacred Magic of Abramelin the Mage*, the *Armadel*, *The Grimoirum Verum*, and the *Grimoire of Honorius*. The best known and most influential were the *Greater* and *Lesser Key of Solomon*. It was the *Lesser Key*, the *Lemegeton* as it was also known, that was most influential. This work listed 72 demonic princes (as compared to the 69 listed by Weyer). For each demon there was a unique seal or sigil, a complex diagram that was used to summon and control it. There is also a description of the appearance the demon had when it first appeared and of other attributes it has. So for example, the demon Baal appears as a cat-headed man with a hoarse voice while Astaroth manifests as a foul angel with stinking breath. The reason for the association with the biblical King Solomon was the medieval Islamic myth about him, according to which he commanded a whole array of demons and compelled them to perform tasks for him (such as building the Temple) by the use of a ring that had the name of God (YHVH) written upon it. The various grimoires were almost all produced in the sixteenth and seventeenth centuries, although they drew upon earlier medieval texts, but they were presented as being much older, hence the claim to authorship by Solomon himself.

Despite the rituals being black magic, intended to evoke demonic powers, they are full of appeals to God and the trinity and Christian powers. There are also detailed accounts of the lengthy preparations including prayers and fasting that the magician had to undergo.

One constant feature was warning about the danger of the rituals, which were described as being difficult and dangerous procedures. Above all, it was vital that the summoner did not step outside his protective circle or allow the demon to escape its confinement in the pentacle since in that event it would almost certainly seize or possess him, with painful death perhaps the least bad outcome. The notion that ritual could be used to control demons derived from the long-standing idea of sorcery or ritual magic when it was applied to the belief in a hierarchy or society of fallen angels, headed by the Devil himself. This was different though from a demonic pact in which the supplicant sold their soul to Satan or entered into an agreement with him, because the idea in theory was for the summoner to control and use the demon as an instrument. (For the way that sorcery was combined with witchcraft to produce the Renaissance witch-craze see Chapter 8). A modern way of understanding these rituals is that the preparation and the rituals themselves, including the words of power that are chanted or declaimed, are a means to create a kind of mental state or focus on the part of the wizard. According to modern occultists the mental state and the psychic energies associated with it will then have an actual effect on the world or events. This leaves open the question of whether the demons that are evoked are simply symbolic representations of particular mental processes and states of mind or are actual beings of some kind.

Demons could affect the world and human beings in a direct and physical way. Although they were spiritual and immaterial beings, they could manifest in physical form and there were various theories as to how they could adopt a tangible and physical body. The commonest was that the physical body was a kind of construct that the demon put together out of raw elements and that it had the same relation to their real existence that clothes did to a person's - in other words, they were like vestments or apparel. It followed from this that they could adopt and appear in any shape or form. Demonology argued that despite this ability (which aided them in deceiving and confusing their victims) each demon had a favoured appearance which was the one it would normally adopt when evoked. One question that had no clear answer was that of whether demons were omnipresent - that is could they be in several different places at the same time? A common answer was that they could, with a common argument being that only that would explain how the Devil could appear in physical form at geographically separate witches sabbats that happened at the same time. The alternative view was that he could only physically be at one and sent representatives (lesser demons) to the others. What was agreed was that all demons, like their master, were not located in a particular place while in their incorporeal form but could be invoked and then adopt physical form in a specific location. Rather confusingly they were also located in the physical reality of Hell but that problem was resolved by the increasing tendency to think of Hell as a state of mind rather than an actual place.

In their physical interactions with the world demons could do all manner of things, most of them harmful such as blighting crops, killing livestock, bringing sickness. There were two particular kinds of interaction with the physical that attracted much attention. One was the phenomenon of demonic sex or seduction. The consensus was that demons themselves were sexless by nature but could adopt the form of either a man or a woman as the circumstances required. A seductive demon in its female form was a succubus, in its male form it was an incubus. In both forms it would lie on top of the victim during sleep, producing a suffocating sensation and either extracting semen (as a succubus) or penetrating the victim and placing semen in them (as an incubus). Demon lovers became a prominent feature of Gothic and modern occult and fantasy fiction but the idea was around before it found expression in literature. It has a number of well-known representations in art such as the works of the painters Henry Fuseli or Nikolaj Abildgaard or the statue *The Succubus* by Rodin. There is a naturalistic explanation for this belief, which is found around the world, in the effects of hypnagogic hallucinations and sleep paralysis or the results of oxygen deprivation due to sleep apnoea.

The other major interaction of demons with the material world was possession. As mentioned above, the idea of spirit possession is a universal one, found in every human culture but it was given a particular twist in Christian thought because of the identification of the 'unclean spirits' found in the New Testament with the demons of satanic rebellion. Since the disciples are recorded as casting out such demons following the descent of the Holy Spirit at Pentecost (and also after Jesus had told them that this was one of the powers he would grant them) churches that accept the doctrine of the apostolic succession such as the Roman Catholic and Orthodox churches (and also the Anglican churches) believe that this is a transmitted power still exercised by priests who are properly ordained. Consequently, exorcism, the Christian ritual for the expulsion of possessing demons, is a recognised procedure, still widely practised by many denominations.

The Renaissance Grimoires were relegated to the back shelves for a while during the eighteenth century but received renewed attention in the nineteenth century. One work that revived interest and created much of the modern iconography of demons was the *Dictionaire Infernal* by the French author and occultist Jacques Collin de Plancy which was first published in 1818, with the famous illustrations being added in 1863. Towards the end of the century and in the early part of the twentieth, several of the major grimoires were translated and reproduced by A. E. Waite and Samuel Liddell MacGregor Mathers. Since then there has been a steady stream of new editions with even the most obscure goetic handbooks now in print. Demonic invocation and possession by demons have both become features of well-known and successful works of film and popular fiction such as *The Exorcist* (based on the novel by William Peter Blatty) and *The Devil Rides Out* by Dennis Wheatley. In works of this kind demons are still seen in the traditional way, as fallen angels and subordinates of the Devil. They also appear in a de-Christianised form in popular television series such as *Charmed* but they are still malevolent, hostile, and dangerous creatures. Very different is the demonology of contemporary authors such as Michael W. Ford and Stephanie Connolly, who take a positive view of demons and their possible uses (in a form of theistic Satanism that believes in the real existence of such entities). Meanwhile in the growing area of chaos magic, demons and the mythology around them are just one of the belief systems that the magician can adopt and use, in a way that makes the question of their existence a secondary one.

As mentioned earlier, Christian thought made all supernatural and magical beings part of the Devil's domain. So, in addition to the legions of demons working alongside him, he had other helpers and assistants in the form of various supernatural creatures. One belief, that he had such helpers in the form of humans who had chosen to enter into a pact with him (witches and warlocks) was so powerful and had such extensive effects, that it has its own chapter. The other beings were never as fully or explicitly integrated into the narrative of the Devil in the way that witches were. They were all creatures of a kind of popular legend found in various forms all over the world and in their European variants remained the characters of a distinct mythology of their own. However, although not explicitly tied to the Devil they were thought of as dark creatures and powers and so part of the larger category of the dark and evil. If not explicitly on the Devil's team they were in some sense allies. Belief in such creatures has tended to evolve in the same way as belief in the Devil; it has declined yet at the same time it has persisted while the decline in serious belief has been combined with both an increase in representation in fiction and literature and a marked revaluation of their moral standing and nature.

The first of these was that of evil or malevolent fairies. As mentioned, Christian orthodoxy would have it that all fairies were a species of minor demon. In popular belief however the 'fair folk' or 'little people' were certainly uncanny, possibly dangerous but not necessarily evil or malevolent. Some, such as the fairy godmother of French fairy narratives, were actively benevolent. The general practice was to make a distinction between good and bad fairies. This was captured in the traditional Scottish distinction between the 'seelie' and unseelie' courts of the realm of the fairies. Some types of fairy such as goblins were almost always thought of as malevolent. One example from Scottish Border folklore was the Redcap, a malevolent sprite or goblin taking the form of "*a short, thickset old man with long prominent teeth, skinny fingers armed with talons like eagles, large eyes of a fiery red colour, grisly hair streaming down his shoulders, iron boots, a pikestaff in his left hand, and a red cap on his head*" (Briggs, 1976). These haunted ruined castles and would waylay and kill unwary travellers, using their blood to dye their caps. Another example was the creature Yallery Brown, found in a Lincolnshire tale, which appeared to provide benefits to the person who found it but actually delivered a lifetime of misfortune and ill luck. Mythical creatures of this kind are not only found on the Eastern side of the Atlantic but also appear in the New World, as for example in the case of the Nain Rouge found in the very prosaic surroundings of Detroit. Apart from the actively spiteful and malevolent fairies there were neutral ones who could still pose a threat to people by such things as abducting them to the realm of faerie where time ran differently or by stealing away children and replacing them with a changeling. (Abduction into faerie was the supposed fate of the Scottish minister Robert Kirk, the author of one of the earliest works on them, *The Secret Commonwealth of Elves, Fauns, and Fairies*).

Perhaps the best-known example of a dark creature that is seen as malevolent but not explicitly linked to the Devil is that of the vampire. The core belief, in the existence of a creature that is undead or immortal, and which subsists by drinking the blood and vitality of living humans, is found in folklore under different names in every part of the world. In Europe it was most widespread in Eastern Europe and the Balkans, the places that are now most associated with it. Thus, it is found as the shtriga in Albanian folklore, and the vrykolak in Greek. The European vampire was always thought of as an undead creature or revenant, that is a corpse that had taken on a form or semblance of life. They were usually described as being of a dark or ruddy complexion, unlike the preternaturally pale vampire of contemporary fiction. This body of folkloric belief entered European higher culture in 1751 when Augustin Calmet published his *Treatise on the Apparitions of Spirits and on Vampires or Revenants: of Hungary, Moravia, et al,* an early work of pioneering folklore study, although Calmet himself seems to have taken the beliefs he recounted seriously. Subsequently the vampire made an appearance in literature including works by figures such as Goethe. In the nineteenth century the vampire became a major feature of popular literature and began to take on the attributes that are now familiar. The breakthrough text in English was *The Vampyre* by John Polidori. The author was the physician of Lord Byron (the vampire of the story, Lord Ruthven, is often taken to be a thinly disguised portrait of Byron himself) and the story was a product of the remarkable story-telling contest that also gave rise to Mary Shelley's *Frankenstein*. (This means that one night of storytelling in nineteenth century Switzerland gave rise to two of the most powerful myths of the contemporary world). The success of Polidori's narrative meant the predatory vampire became a feature of popular Victorian fiction, in such works as the splendidly over the top *Varney the Vampire: or the Feast of Blood* from 1847. Later there was the much higher quality *Carmilla* by Joseph Sheridan LeFanu and the novel that has now come to define the concept for many, *Dracula* by Bram Stoker.

In the twentieth century vampire narratives that drew on Stoker became a prominent feature of film and later television. In these initially the vampire was presented in what had become the canonical fashion, as a malevolent and hostile creature, predatory and almost certainly damned. They were not explicitly connected to the Devil but were certainly agents of the forces of darkness. The last few decades of the century and the start of the present one has seen a remarkable shift in the portrayal and moral evaluation of the vampire, starting with the *Vampire Chronicles* of Anne Rice. In these the vampire becomes at least morally ambiguous, an antihero or romantic villain, but increasingly a positive figure. This has now led to a veritable industry of series of novels by authors such as Laurel Hamilton, Stephanie Meyer, and J. R. Ward, to give just three examples. All of these have been very popular and, in several cases, have led to success in other media such as film. The revaluation of the vampire in these works (as well as other creatures such as the werewolf and the witch) clearly parallels the similar revaluation of the Devil that we can see, although it is less marked in his case. Partly this reflects the way the supernatural has come to be seen in a different light with the decline of Christianity and Christian theology as intellectual and cultural influences. It is now seen as risky or dangerous but also fascinating and potentially good or at least morally neutral. There is also the persistent theme of the apparently supernatural actually being a part of a wider, natural order. The popularity of these kinds of work suggests that they are a way of exploring and dealing with issues that have come to the fore in contemporary culture, above all individualism and sexuality and the issues that these now raise for identity. Since the demonic, in the shape of the Devil and the wider category of demons, is one way of thinking about particular aspects of human nature, we may anticipate that demons will also undergo this kind of process of partial revaluation.

The other main folkloric creature that is associated with radical evil and the power of darkness is the werewolf. As with vampirism, the notion of certain apparently normal human beings who can shift into animal form is a widespread one. (The wolf is the common one in Europe but, for obvious reasons, it is other species that occur in the folklore in other parts of the world, such as the jaguar in Mexico and the fox in Japan). Sometimes the transformation is automatic and uncontrolled, triggered by events or circumstances outside the control of the person while in other cases it is something that can be done at will. This is a powerful metaphor for the suppressed or denied animal nature and urges of human beings, a denial of the idea of humanism or human exceptionalism that is a core element of many religious traditions, particularly the monotheistic ones. In much of the world the wolf has become a signifier or symbol of the violent and predatory side of human nature, making the werewolf or *loup garou* a powerful metaphor for this.

In its original form, which persisted for a long time, lycanthropy, the shifting from human to wolf, was a kind of condition or curse that was unsought and not directly chosen by the person involved. This did not mean that those suspected of it were treated gently because they were also seen as savage and dangerous and fit only for putting down – it was just that the element of guilt or moral blame was absent. There were traditional remedies for the condition, the main drawback being that many of them were fatal. During the Renaissance and Reformation however, this belief was combined with the idea of collaboration with the Devil and the notion took root that it was a chosen fate, deriving from a conscious choice to work for the side of darkness and the Evil One (although the idea that a bite from a werewolf in its lupine form could transmit the condition, on the analogy of rabies, persisted). As a result, there were several witch trials that involved accusations of lycanthropy alongside the more common ones.

With the decline in elite belief in the witch-cult the werewolf tended to revert to its earlier folkloric form in the eighteenth century but the presentation of werewolves as evil, predatory creatures persisted. In the nineteenth and twentieth century the ideas became part of the emergent genres of horror fiction and film and as with vampires several of the commonly associated features of the werewolf appeared at that time. One such was the belief that they could only be killed by silver weapons or bullets. For most of the twentieth century werewolves were portrayed in two ways; sometimes (as in the famous 1941 film, *The Wolfman*) as tragic figures with an uncontrollable urge or process that caused anguish and despair but could not be resisted, on other occasions as evil and in control of their fate (as in the novel *The Howling*). Increasingly the second kind of story presented the werewolf as sinister but darkly romantic and fascinating (as for example in the 1994 film *Wolf*) and this in turn prefigured a revaluation of the moral status of werewolves similar to that of vampires. An early example of this was the 1948 novel *Darker Than You Think*, by Jack Williamson, but later with the works of authors such as Stephanie Meyer werewolves become heroic characters. As with vampires this indicated a rethinking of Christian ways of understanding human nature and an exploration of what this might mean.

The Devil is thus only the central figure in a wider array of dark beings and entities, in the traditional Christian conception of his nature and role. These entities may be directly connected to him, as demons and witches are, or they may be independent, aspects of the pre-Christian beliefs of the population that survived the efforts of the Churches to eradicate them. In all cases though, even if the creatures in question were not seen as explicitly and openly being the devil's servants, they were on the same side as him and shared his qualities of evil, malevolence, and opposition to virtue and the good. As the modern world has progressed the feelings of fear and horror once associated with demons, evil spirits, revenants and creatures such as vampires and werewolves have been transferred to other things and the whole 'dark side' has begun to be reinterpreted, with the aspects of human natures that myths such as those of demons and werewolves represented, increasingly seen as aspects of a more complex human nature, maybe regrettable but natural and increasingly as morally ambiguous or even admirable.

Further Reading

Bane, Theresa (2012) *Encyclopedia of Demons in World Religions and Cultures*. McFarland.

Boyd, Katie (2009) *Devils and Demonology in the 21st Century*. Schiffer.

Briggs, Katherine (1976) *A Dictionary of Fairies*. Penguin.

Connolly, Stephanie (2006) *The Complete Book of Demonolatry*. DB Publishing.

Davies, Owen (2010) *Grimoires: A History of Magic Books*. Oxford University Press.

Gettings, Fred (1988) *Dictionary of Demons: A Guide to Demons and Demonologists in Occult Lore*. Guild Publishing.

Greer, John Michael (2011, 1st published 2001) *Monsters*. Llewellyn.

Groom, Nick (2020) *The Vampire: A New History*. Yale University Press.

Guiley, Rosemary Ellen (2005) *The Encyclopedia of Vampires, Werewolves, and Other Monsters*. Checkmark Books.

Guiley, Rosemary Ellen (2009) *The Encyclopedia of Demons & Demonology*. Checkmark Books.

Izzard, John (2009) *Werewolves*. Octopus Publishing.

Jones, David Albert (2011) *Angels: A Very Short Introduction*. Oxford University Press.

Langton, Edward (2014, 1st published 1949) *Essentials of Demonology: A Study of Jewish and Christian Doctrine, Its Origin and Development*. Wipf and Stock.

Mack, Carol K. and Dinah. (1998) *A Field Guide to Demons, Fairies, Fallen Angels, and Other Subversive Spirits*. Henry Holt.

Mathers, S. L. MacGregor (trans.) (1975, 1st published 1900) *The Book of the Sacred Magic of Abramelin the Mage*. Dover.

Mathers, S. L. MacGregor (trans.) (2001) *The Grimoire of Armadel*. Weiser.

Mathers, S. L. MacGregor (trans.) (2000, 1st published 1889) *The Key of Solomon the King*. Weiser.

Mathers, S. L. MacGregor and Crowley, Aleister (trans. and ed.) (1995) *The Goetia: The Lesser Key of Solomon the King*. Weiser.

Otten, Charlotte (ed.) (1986) *A Lycanthropy Reader: Werewolves in Western Culture*. Syracuse University Press.

de Plancy, Colin (2019) *The Infernal Dictionary: Devils, Gods, and Spirits of the Dictionaire Infernal*. Independently Published.

Robbins, Rossell Hope (2015) *The Encyclopedia of Witchcraft and Demonology*. Girard & Stewart.

Summers, Montague (2003, 1st published 1933) *The Werewolf in Lore and Legend*. Dover.

Summers, Montague (2009) *Vampires and Vampirism*. Dover.

Summers, Montague (2001) *The Vampire in Lore and Legend*. Dover.

Taylor, Joules (2009) *Vampires*. Octopus Publishing

Weyer, Johann (2017, 1st published 1583) *Pseudomonarchia Daemonum: The False Monarchy of Demons*. CreateSpace.

Chapter 8. The Devil's Servants: Witches, Warlocks, and Witch Hunts

People from all parts of the world and all periods of history have believed in the existence and power of witches. Many continue to do so. The forms this belief takes are varied but there are also recurrent elements. What is not often realised is that the Western idea of the witch is different in important ways from the wider belief, ways that led to one of the great moral panics and witch hunts (a literal one in this case). Until the later Middle Ages the peoples of Christian Europe had a set of beliefs about witches and witchcraft that were not that much different from those found elsewhere but at that point something novel was introduced. This novel element was the combining of traditional folkloric beliefs with the idea of the Devil, making witches willing collaborators with, and servants of, the Devil. Part of this process was a transference to the figure of the witch of a kind of obsessive fantasy that had recurred throughout Christian history. This combination led to what we can now see clearly was a massive outbreak of panic and hysteria, with disastrous results. We should not be too self-congratulatory for our greater enlightenment, however. More recent events show that the underlying fantasy still has power and a hold on the minds of many people and needs only the right circumstances to burst out again.

The idea of witchcraft as a quality or practice is found in almost every human culture as is belief in those who practice it, witches (of both sexes). The common beliefs are these. Firstly, that there are magical skills, rituals, and practices that work and can be used for both good and ill. Some bring benefits such as finding things that are lost, curing illness or preventing it, winning love and in general assuring good fortune. Others bring harm and ill fortune. The witch is a person who can do this. Secondly, that the ability to work this magic for either purpose is an inherent or inherited ability. Some people have it while most do not. Sometimes the ability is seen as being as much an unchosen curse as an ability – this was a common view of what was known as the 'sight' for example (meaning the ability to see visions of the future or things that were part of the realm of the magical and which most people could not perceive). In some cases, the idea is that the witch can bring about effects, particularly harmful ones, without consciously intending to do so or willing it. In such cases they work their magic at an unconscious level. This belief is found in Europe (and in Indo-European folklore generally) in the shape of the belief in the 'evil eye', the idea that some people have an inborn capacity which means that if they look upon another person or their possessions in an envious or covetous fashion, bad consequences will follow for the person or thing so regarded. In such cases there is no active ill-will on the part of the person causing the harm. In other cases though, there may well be conscious intention, worked through a mechanism such as a curse or charm.

Beliefs of this kind and associated ones such as that in charms or amulets that bring good luck and protect against bad fortune and the effects of spells or magic used with ill intent, are universal and tremendously varied. The crucial point for this discussion is that the people who work the magic, witches of either sex, have no connection to a malevolent and evil higher power and have not gained their ability through any kind of compact or agreement: usually they are born with it, sometimes it is acquired by study. This kind of belief was a part of European folklore for centuries, both before and after the coming of Christianity. In the British Isles this took the form of 'cunning' men and women, people who were known in their community for having magical abilities and were turned to for assistance in dealing with life's difficulties – and also, sometimes, for darker purposes. The same pattern can be found throughout Europe. This was generally a feature of peasant and lower-class rather than elite culture but many among the upper classes were not averse to employing cunning men and women or consulting fortune-tellers.

The attitude of the Church to this was clear but very different from what it would later become. The orthodox view was that folk magic of this kind was a superstition and also a snare or delusion because it stopped people from relying upon God and trusting him. Magic and divination therefore had no actual effect. The teaching was that the Devil was ultimately responsible for this but only inasmuch as he had created this delusion or false belief to lead people astray. Witches were deluded people who had been deceived by the Devil into thinking that they had actual effective powers. They had also been deluded into believing that they experienced the so-called 'ride of Diana' in which they were able to fly through the sky in the train of the goddess of the hunt, Diana or Artemis. The views of the Church were embodied in a canon, part of the canon law of the Church, known as the Canon *Episcopi* (from its opening passage). It laid a duty on bishops and senior clergy to discourage belief of this kind and to punish both people who resorted to witches, and the witches themselves. The emphasis throughout was on the false and ultimately imaginary nature of the powers, experiences, and effects – hardly surprising since they were invented as a trick by the Father of Lies.

Simultaneously the Church did believe in the reality and effectiveness of sorcery. This belief, which was inherited from the late ancient world, was that rituals of certain kinds could bring about the manifestation and appearance of supernatural or divine beings. For the Church this was effective but damnable and blasphemous, because it involved the appeal to the Devil or to entities now identified as demonic, and therefore fallen angels like him. Sorcery was clearly distinguished from witchcraft however. This can be seen in the treatment of the two by the judicial system at that time. Charges of using charms or employing magic were prosecuted as breaches of Christian practice and succumbing to superstition, usually involved members of the lower classes, and brought light punishment (usually a penance). The exception was cases where the witch was supposed to have practised maleficium (evil working) i.e. bringing about evil results by magic. This was punished more severely but because of the belief in the inefficacy and illusory nature of witchcraft, the punishment was for intention rather than actual action. The practice of ritual sorcery by contrast was a grave charge that led to the death penalty if proven (because it was a species of heresy) and such trials were rare and almost always involved members of the elite (as for example in the notorious case of Gilles de Rais). One reason for sorcery trials and charges only involving members of the elite was that the practice of sorcery required education and literacy, which the mass of the population did not have. The rarity of the charges reflected a number of factors but mainly the reality that this was a highly private activity (it was hardly something that could be done publicly or in a way that became public knowledge) and this made it both hard to prove and difficult to detect and then charge. (It was also almost certainly very rare).

All of this changed in the tumultuous period that followed the Black Death. Christian Europe's thinking about witchcraft underwent a dramatic change, and the nature of the beliefs held about it shifted radically. This intellectual movement took place mainly among the elite (at least initially) and this was the reason why the change had such a marked effect, not least on the workings of the criminal justice system. A simple way of understanding the change is to say that the formerly distinct ideas of witchcraft and sorcery were combined but the process requires more unpacking. The origins of the shift lie in two things: a kind of recurrent fantasy that recurs regularly in the history of Western and Catholic Europe (interestingly not so much in Eastern or Orthodox Europe), and an institution set up for practical reasons but which was often moved by that fantasy.

The fantasy was the belief that underneath the respectable surface of society was a hidden underground conspiracy of people devoted to evil ideas and looking to subvert all of the Christian order. This underground conspiracy was always thought of as engaging in all kinds of monstrous practices and rituals, above all ones that involved the ritual debasement and murder of unbaptised infants. Its basically anti-Christian nature meant that it was also utterly blasphemous, with rituals and practices that were parodies of Christian ones and deliberate blasphemous attacks on them. This fantasy, of an underground conspiracy or cult of baby killers and evil workers, was associated with the Devil and worship of him (or at least as being inspired and directed by him) because in a Christian society there can be no worse thing than to be a servant of the Devil. All kinds of groups became associated with this notion. Among the earliest were Jews and stories of this kind about Jews were a recurrent feature of anti-Semitic outbreaks in Medieval Europe – this was the origin of the myth of Jews using the blood of unbaptised infants to make Passover wafers. It was also the central feature of the allegations made against the Knights Templar, during the suppression of the Order by Philip the Fair of France. It also became a regular feature of allegations against heretics. Thus, accusations of this kind were made against the Cathars, the Manichee cult that became widely established in Southern France in the twelfth century, before being exterminated in the savage Albigensian Crusade of 1209 to 1229.

At the same time the Church responded to the threat of heresies such as Catharism by creating the Holy Office for the Doctrine of the Faithful or, as it is better known, the Inquisition. In its origins the intention behind the Inquisition was twofold: to combat heresy but also to mitigate the severity of the law. Heresy was a secular charge that attracted the death penalty and the aim was to make the treatment of these charges more rigorous and protect people from malicious accusations. In the aftermath of the fourteenth century heresies of all kinds became more widespread and the Inquisition more active – these movements (such as the Beghards, and Brethren of the Free Spirit) also attracted the kind of fantastical charges mentioned above. The Inquisition developed a procedure to deal with accusations of heresy, which involved protections for the accused but also the use of torture to extract confessions. This was to deal with the problem of prosecuting a crime that was covert and private and where, often, there were no witnesses.

At this point, in the fifteenth century, the fatal amendment was made. Theologians who had developed a method for dealing with heresy and an image of what a heretical underground looked like, applied that model to witchcraft. Instead of being a matter of individual deluded or fantasising women it became an underground sect of heretics. This meant they became devil worshippers. The crucial jump was to then believe that the powers they claimed or were thought to have were real and actual. Where though did they come from? The obvious answer, given the fantasy, was that they came from the Devil. This fitted with the increasing fear of him and his power that was a marked feature of the intellectual history of that time (the fifteenth and sixteenth centuries). The central part of this new way of thinking about witches was the notion of a demonic pact. The idea was that witches were people (the majority women but many men as well) who had entered into an engagement or pact with the Devil. By this they undertook to serve him and worship him and in return he gave them magical powers – since however they came from him, they could be used only to do evil. The witch thus transitioned from being a deluded or fantasising person to an active servant and collaborator of the Devil. The fantasy of an underground conspiracy meant that they were no longer solitary but part of an organised counter-society – where there was one witch there had to be more. Where though did they meet, if they were organised? The material conditions of society at the time meant that there were few places where people could meet in private unless they were elite, and often not even then. The solution was to say that they met in remote or desolate places, away from prying eyes. How though did they get there? To resolve this, the Inquisitors reversed another position and argued that the narratives of 'night-flying' were actually true and that witches could indeed fly through the night using things such as a magical ointment, the secret of which was given to them by the Devil. They used this ability to gather in collective sabbats, blasphemous parodies of Christian rituals, in places like mountaintops and heathlands. (The details of the sabbats were the same as those in the allegations made earlier against people such as the Templars and heretics). Thus, the ideas of witchcraft and sorcery had been conflated, with the witches now supposedly engaging in the kinds of rituals that constituted sorcery, all as followers of the ultimate heresy – that of serving and worshipping the Devil.

This new view appeared suddenly in writings from the 1430s. It was novel but made use of ideas about the Devil and his nature that went back to St Augustine. Initially this idea, that witches were a conspiracy, was a minority one but it received official approval from the Papacy with the Bull *Summis Desiderantes Affectibus*, issued by Innocent VIII in 1484. What this led to was firstly investigations of accused witches by inquisitors and secondly the incorporation of many popular myths and superstitions about magic and witchcraft into the new picture the inquisitors had created. This found expression in the first, and most influential, of the witch hunting manuals, the *Malleus Maleficarum* of Heinrich Kremer, published in 1486. This was a compendium of a whole array of folk motifs and beliefs, which were incorporated into and made compatible with the new official theology and understanding of witchcraft as a species of Devil worship and the witch as a willing servant of the Devil. The aim was to root out and exterminate witches wherever they might be found. This had a dramatic effect and the *Malleus* was one of the most influential books ever written in terms of its impact. The reason was this: previously, while the common people had believed in the reality and efficacy of magic and witchcraft (both harmful and helpful) the elite in general had not. Now, the elite and particularly the lower levels of the upper classes, came very rapidly to believe in the newly created witch-myth. This mattered because they were the people who controlled the lower levels of the criminal justice system – they were the 'gatekeepers' who decided whether accusations should be taken seriously or not. Previously accusations of causing harm by witchcraft were not taken that seriously but now they were.

Moreover, if an accusation was taken seriously it now triggered an investigation employing the techniques and procedures developed by the Inquisition to deal with heretics. The result was catastrophic. It triggered a witch hunt that would rage across large parts of Europe for two centuries. This was a literal witch hunt but it is important to realise that events of this kind are a regular and inevitable result of the workings of the criminal justice system, as subsequent events have shown. You can have a witch hunt, analytically speaking even when the crime in question is not the literal one of witchcraft. In the abstract witch hunts work this way. The starting point is a moral panic, a sociological phenomenon in which many people, including those with power, are gripped by an anxiety or panic about some kind of activity that is supposed to be morally repulsive and to pose a serious threat to society. If this is something treated as a crime (as it usually is) the result is a sharp increase in investigation and prosecution. Sometimes though the crime is a private one where there are few or no witnesses or it is a conspiratorial one, engaged in by a covert organisation. In that case it becomes very difficult to prosecute using the usual procedures of the criminal justice system, which have extensive protections for the accused to prevent wrongful convictions. The solution is to rely upon confessions, often extracted by dubious means. These confessions typically incriminate people other than the original suspects and so the result is an escalating cascade of cases, which makes the panic even worse.

This is exactly what happened with witchcraft after the 1480s. We have an abundance of records from the literally thousands of trials that took place over the two centuries or more after 1484. These all show common features and have a remarkably similar structure and content. The reason for this was the way investigators all over Europe employed a similar procedure. The initial event was always a charge of complaint against an individual, of harm supposedly brought about by magic. This would now be taken seriously by the magistrate (a member of the local elite, now convinced of the real existence and powers of witches, as servants of the Devil). The accused would be arrested and questioned. In most of Europe this involved the use of torture, particularly sustained sleep deprivation. There was a standard questionnaire that was used everywhere with the same questions in the same order, which is why the confessions all contained the same elements and had the same structure. The questions can be reconstructed from the answers but we also have surviving witch hunters' manuals (the *Malleus* was only the first of many) which set them out. The questions were leading ones of the "Have you stopped beating your wife?" variety and the first one was always "When and how did you first meet the Devil?" soon followed by "How did you enter into a pact with him and what happened?". The critical ones that turned the individual case into a mass one were "When did you go to a Sabbat?" and "Who else was there?" The accused, under torture and highly suggestible or even hallucinating from sleep deprivation, would come up with all kinds of story to satisfy their questioners and, crucially, would name and implicate many of their neighbours. They would be arrested and questioned in their turn and the result was a cascade of cases that produced mutually supportive and interlocking confessions (because the subsequent arrestees would be questioned in ways that referred to and incorporated earlier confessions). All of this made the belief in a conspiracy of Devil-worshipping witches seem true and so added to the panic.

The obvious result was that in many parts of Europe there were mass trials, with dozens of people arrested, the great majority of whom would be executed in the manner prescribed for heretics, burning at the stake. Not all parts of Europe experienced the mania to the same degree: the Iberian Peninsula and Italy escaped lightly whereas Germany, Scotland and parts of France suffered badly. In many parts of Europe, the great majority of those accused were women but there was always a significant minority of men and in some areas such as Scandinavia, the Baltic Lands and Russia men were the majority. As a legal and sociological phenomenon, it has attracted much attention and has generated a massive scholarship. The main interest here is the cultural impact of the hunts and trials and the way they fed into contemporary ideas about the Devil and also created a distinct mythology of witchcraft, found nowhere else in the world. The theologians and inquisitors who had put together the initial account of witchcraft in the 1430s had drawn on classical accounts of the powers of the Devil and demons and their ability to act physically in the world. They had also taken ideas found in both classical antiquity and popular belief and reversed the presumption of scepticism as to their reality. What the trials did was to incorporate masses of folk beliefs into the confessions and records, as accused people drew upon local folklore to provide content for the confessions they were forced to produce. All this combined with the theology to produce a new kind of picture and narrative of witchcraft. This in turn then fed back into the investigations and questions put to accused and so set up a self-sustaining feedback in which the trials generated a mythology that then drove more trials and investigations and was written up in learned treatises and witch hunters manuals.

The resulting picture is a familiar one. The Devil, seeking always to subvert and overthrow Christianity, was always looking for willing helpers. These could be found among the poor and desperate, the outcast and marginal, but also the elite and ambitious. He, or his agents, could appear in bodily form to the candidate when their insight told them the time was right. In confessions the accused gave accounts of how the Devil had suddenly appeared to them, sometimes as an animal but more often as a man of short stature wearing black clothes (often called John for some reason). He would then offer them a deal in which they received the power to work magic and get vengeance on those who had slighted them, in return for becoming his servants and worshippers. The deal would be consummated by the Devil placing his 'mark' on the witch by biting them, producing a spot that was incapable of sensation. He would then have sex with them with the sex often described as painful – accounts also mentioned that his semen was ice cold. It was this, the demonic pact, that made the practice of magic into heresy and a crime subject to the death penalty but the meeting with the Devil was always private, hence the need for confessions. The witch would then be put in contact with the others in her locality and join the conspiracy. At regular intervals she would travel to gatherings or sabbats with other witches. These would involve veneration of and sex with the Devil or his emissary, often marked by the 'shameful kiss' i.e. kissing his anus, together with indiscriminate sex in general. There would also be human sacrifice, of unbaptised infants, that would then be eaten so making witches participants in both infanticide and cannibalism (the two actions that signify utter barbarity and moral turpitude in both classical and Christian thought).

Confessions also contained detailed accounts of specific instances of maleficium or evil working by magic means. These included things such as blighting crops, causing accidents to happen to people, killing livestock, bringing sickness, and bewitching people in various ways (causing impotence or barrenness was a common one). In folk belief it had always been thought that magic could do these things or protect against them but now the emphasis was all on the causing side. Above all, these actions were now seen as being done for and at the behest of, the Devil, as part of his unceasing war against the good. He, rather than the witch, was the motivator. This meant that while often there is a clear possible motive (revenge for being slighted or denied alms for example) more often the harmful magic is motivated by pure malice and delight in destruction, reflecting its ultimate source. All of this both derived from and fed into and strengthened, the Renaissance and Reformation era's fear of the Devil and growing belief in his power and ability to act in the world. Not only was he more of a psychological threat, the witch cult meant that he had a vast army of physical servants all committed to his cause and doing his work, and doing all this in secret. This meant he could act in the world in a far more effective way and made him seem more menacing and all-pervading than ever. For those two and a half centuries, from the middle of the fifteenth to the early eighteenth century, the existence of a cult of witches bound to the Devil by a demonic pact, was a major part of the conception of the Devil and his doings. At the same time it created and consolidated a folk myth of great power, that of the witch.

Eventually though the panic faded and the trials petered out, in the early decades of the eighteenth century. There had always been sceptics, who adhered to the older belief that witchcraft was certainly an invention of the Devil, but as a snare or delusion that led people astray (so making the witch trials and persecutions and the suspicion and fear they engendered his goal). These included people such as Johan Weyer, who as we saw earlier, was a great believer in demons but not in witches. Another was the sixteenth century English writer Reginald Scott whose *Discoverie of Witchcraft* published in 1584 is both an attack on the belief and a setting out of its main elements. For many years though the sceptics were in the minority (there were such sceptics in all of the denominations) and outweighed by the proponents of the witch-belief, who included the major political theorist Jean Bodin, and James VI of Scotland, who wrote a major scholarly tome on witchcraft and demonology. Eventually however elite opinion wearied of the bloodshed and suffering attendant on the trials and became alienated by the increasingly bizarre claims and confessions. This also went along with a more general weariness with religious enthusiasm and fanaticism that took hold among many of the elites in the final decade of the seventeenth century and the first two of the eighteenth. In addition, one feature of the trials had always been that the explosively growing arrests in a major outbreak had come to a fairly abrupt halt when accusations began to be aimed at members of the upper classes, or when the national elite became involved. By the middle of the eighteenth century, although individual members of the upper classes continued to believe in the existence of the witch cult, it was very much a minority view and no longer respectable.

Amongst the lower classes however, the belief in witches as described by the myth that had formed in the fifteenth century had now become settled, and it persisted there for far longer. As such this was a part of the way belief in the magical and supernatural and also in the power and activity of a personal Devil survived in force in those parts of society when it had declined among most of the formally educated. Because the gatekeepers to the criminal justice system, local elites and magistrates, were now more sceptical (and not supported by their superiors) legal witch hunts did not happen, because the crucial initial step of taking an accusation seriously and acting on it by arresting a subject and interrogating them in a fixed style no longer happened. We should not though be self-congratulatory about our superior rationality and humaneness. Exactly the same mechanisms and processes have happened repeatedly and in at least one case on the basis of a very similar kind of belief and in supposedly enlightened countries, specifically the United States and other countries such as the United Kingdom. This was the great Satanic Abuse panic of the 1980s and early 1990s. It may not have led to actual burnings at the stake but its results were still very severe for those caught up in it. Moreover, it was driven by beliefs uncannily like those of three hundred years earlier.

In the late 1970s there was a rising panic in the US and UK over the sexual abuse of children. This came from two contrasting sources, social conservatives opposed to the cultural trends of the time and radical feminists who believed that aggressive and predatory sexual behaviour by men in the context of the family was being massively underreported. At this point a new element came into play, in the shape of so-called 'repressed' memories. The idea was that people who had experienced a traumatic event, such as abuse while a child, would supress the memory of it so that they would have no conscious recollection of it. However, these memories could be 'recovered' by therapy. What followed was autobiographical accounts of supposed childhood trauma by survivors. One of the ones that attracted the most attention was *Michelle Remembers* by Michelle Smith and her therapist and later husband Lawrence Pazder, published in 1980. In this she claimed that as a child she had been subjected to sustained ritualistic abuse of a sadistic and sexual nature by an underground satanic cult active in Victoria, Canada where she lived and around the world. This underground cult was explicitly devoted to Devil worship (he supposedly appeared in bodily form at the end of one 81-day long ritual that she remembered after therapy). The book created an enormous sensation and soon led to other, similar accounts being published which were publicised by mass media outlets such as the Oprah Winfrey Show.

The result was that very rapidly the idea took hold, mainly initially in conservative and fundamentalist religious circles, that there was an enormous and thousand years old secret conspiracy of devil-worshippers all over the world, practising rituals involving infanticide and cannibalism and the ritual sexual abuse and torture of children, and with members among the apparently respectable, including the wealthy and elite. The similarities with the witch beliefs and the earlier accusations against Jews and heretics are remarkable and obvious. The allegations in books like *Michelle Remembers* and others were taken seriously, despite their being impossible to prove and in many cases either incredibly unlikely or simply impossible (quite apart from scepticism about the central claim of the reality and power of a physical Devil). Why though were they taken seriously? Apart from the way media work the main reason was that one element of the stories, that of ritual and sexual abuse of children, fitted in with a rising anxiety about that topic being created by other groups, typically with no interest in the idea of satanism but a shared belief that serious mistreatment of children was widespread or even common and underreported or even actively concealed. Soon the allegations attracted support from social work professionals and child psychiatrists and came to enter the practice of social work through their being highlighted in in-service training for professionals. This meant that accusations of a child being abused by an underground cult of Satanists were taken seriously by many contemporary 'gatekeepers' for the criminal justice system, such as social workers and child welfare officers, junior police officers and prosecutors.

The outcome was a series of trials and investigations throughout the 1980s and early 1990s, on both sides of the Atlantic. The first one, which attracted major interest, was the trial in 1983–1990 of two people who ran a pre-school in Los Angeles (the McMartin case). To date this remains the longest and most expensive criminal trial in the entire history of the United States. Within a few years similar allegations had been made against over a hundred preschools or day care centres in the US. The idea of Satanic ritual abuse then spread to other countries with similar cases in the UK in Ayrshire, Rochdale, Orkney and Nottingham. The cases involved the use of leading questions and investigative techniques that essentially led children to construct a narrative that fitted the expectations of their questioners, in the same way that interrogations had worked in classic witch trials (minus the physical torture!). The result for innocent families caught up in this hysteria was catastrophic with families broken up and people facing long trials and in some cases imprisonment on the basis of what were later admitted to be spurious charges. In some cases genuine serious sexual abuse was not dealt with properly because investigators were distracted by the allegations of Satanic abuse. Eventually official reports commissioned by agencies such as the Home Office in the UK and the FBI in the US discredited the entire panic. The belief though persists in certain religious circles – it is the official support that has ceased.

This sad experience shows several things. The main one is that the belief in the Devil as an actual person who also has willing and conscious helpers and assistants is very tenacious. In the Middle Ages it was an occasional charge laid against people who had fallen foul of Popes and monarchs (e.g. the unfortunate Templars) or were deviants in some way (Jews and heretics). From the middle of the fifteenth century onwards it took the work of combining the idea of a demonic conspiracy with the folk beliefs in witchcraft and magic. That subsided but still retains currency among some religious believers, particularly, but not exclusively among evangelical Protestants, in the US and elsewhere. At the same time this idea can become combined with other panics and anxieties and when this leads to interaction with the criminal justice system the results are seriously bad. There is a widespread feeling, it would seem, that the way things are is the result of a secret conspiracy by malign and ill-intentioned and also powerful people rather than accident or incompetence. (It seems people would rather believe that the world is run by utterly evil and amazingly competent people rather than that the people who purport to be in charge are actually not in control of much and generally are incompetent and do not know what they are doing – that seems to be the really scary option). There is also a stunningly persistent idea that things are going to hell and that all kinds of bad things are pervasive and getting worse. Both of these outlooks are receptive ground for the idea that all of this is the work of the ultimate conspirator and source of evil – the Devil. The belief that he has collaborators and that they can be identified is where practical trouble really starts, as both recent and older history shows.

On the other hand, things can and do change. The recent history of witchcraft, or at least the idea of it, is a classic illustration of this. During the very late nineteenth and early twentieth century there was a surge in interest in occultism and the magical of all kinds. At the same time anthropologists began to seriously study the folk beliefs and magical practices of people all around the world while historians started to apply historical scholarship to the history of both witch beliefs and the great witch hunt. This led to the appearance of a kind of pseudo-history, in which there actually was a witch cult but not the one of the fervid imaginations of the inquisitors. Instead, the theory was put forward by Margaret Murray and others, that there was a kind of hidden underground religion practised during the Christian centuries and that this consisted of a survival and transmission of older pagan rituals and beliefs, which the Church interpreted as Devil worship. For Murray part of this was the worship of the 'horned god', identified with the Celtic deity Cerunnos. Similar arguments were made by others such as the French romantic historian Jules Michelet in *Witchcraft and Sorcery* and the American folklorist Charles Godfrey Leland in his *Aradia: the Gospel of the Witches*. This meant that there had been an underground anti-Christian faith but it was reinterpreted in a positive way. This fitted in with the appearance at that time of neo-paganism and also the revaluation of both magic in general and the Devil in particular. The next step was for this supposed underground religion to be revived. In fact, there is no evidence that there was such an underground religion (Murray's theories having been thoroughly debunked) but this did not stop people from claiming that it had existed and that in fact they were initiates of it who had decided to come into the open and so revive it as a public, rather than a hidden, practice.

The key figure here was the British civil servant Gerald Gardner who claimed to have been initiated into a coven of the traditional underground cult in the 1930s. Regardless of what we think of that, it is undoubtedly true that he set up his own coven and 'revival' of this in the 1940s and went on to organise and publicise it, particularly after the repeal of the Witchcraft Act in 1951. He was soon followed by other, independent figures, such as Charles Cardell, Cecil Williamson, Sybil Leek, and Alex Sanders. There was inevitably a lot of sensationalist coverage in the media but in the 1960s and 1970s this emergent 'new religion' benefitted from association with the counterculture of that decade. Since the 1970s it has grown rapidly and spread to many parts of the world, so that Wicca (as it is now called) has become a small but dynamic and recognised religion. Like pagan revivalism such as Asatru it claims to be a continuation or revival of an old pagan religion or spirituality but unlike them it almost certainly does not refer to an actually historically existing religion and practice. Instead it is an 'invented tradition' (one of many in the modern world) in which the myth of the witch cult put together by inquisitors and given detail by the actual experience of the witch trials is reinterpreted and made into a positive and benign nature religion. That said, it is still explicitly anti-Christian and rejects not just Christian theology but also much of the social and ethical teaching of the church (while being rather conventional in some ways). Part of the reinterpretation is that the Devil is no longer present, he has been replaced by the figure of the horned god along with the (more significant) triple goddess.

Despite that, we can still connect the appearance and success of Wicca with other cultural changes of the last hundred years such as the revaluation of the Devil and his transformation into a positive figure, that was mentioned in the previous chapter. What is common to both is the rejection of the Christian structure that still shapes Western thought even after formal belief has perished – hence the persistence of Christian themes such as apocalypticism among staunch non-believers. This goes along with a rejection of the monotheistic view of the relation between humanity and the natural order and a significant revaluation of ethics and morality. There is actually a deeper rejection of the whole approach of monotheism, which originated over two thousand years ago in the Middle East and has since spread to every part of the world. In the case of the witch a myth that grew out of the idea of an adversary that is an important part of monotheism has been given a radically new twist, similar to the way that creatures such as the vampire and the werewolf have been reinvented in popular culture, but more profound. The even more radical move is to take the central idea of the Adversary, the Devil himself and either deconstruct it or even reverse it so that he becomes the venerated rather than the abhorred. In the second half of the twentieth century, this is precisely what happened.

Further Reading

Baroja, Julio Caro (2001) *The World of the Witches*. Orion.

Cohn, Norman (1993, 1st published 1975) *Europe's Inner Demons: The Demonization of Christians in Medieval Christendom*. Pimlico.

Davies, Owen (2003) *Cunning Folk: Popular Magic in English History*. Hambledon Continuum.

Davies, Owen (2017) *The Oxford Illustrated History of Witchcraft*. Oxford University Press.

Demos, John (2008). *Enemy Within: 2,000 Years of Witch-Hunting in the Western World*. Viking.

Eberle, Paul & Shirley (1993) *The Abuse of Innocence: the McMartin Preschool Trial*. Prometheus Books.

Frankfurter, David (2006). *Evil Incarnate: Rumours of Demonic Conspiracy and Satanic Abuse in History*. Princeton University Press.

Gaskill, Malcolm (2010). *Witchcraft: A Very Short Introduction*. Oxford University Press.

Greenwood, Susan (2003) *Contemporary Magic and Witchcraft: A Comprehensive Examination of Modern Western Magic*. Amess Publishing.

Greenwood, Susan (2002) *The Encyclopedia of Magic and Witchcraft: An Illustrated Historical Reference to Spiritual Worlds*. Amess Publishing.

Guazzo, Francesca Maria (1988, 1st published 1608) *Compendium Maleficarum*. Dover.

Ellis, Bill (2000) *Raising the Devil: Satanism, New Religions, and the Media*. University Press of Kentucky.

Ellis, Bill (2004) *Lucifer Ascending: The Occult in Folklore and Popular Culture*. University Press of Kentucky.

Hughes, Pennethorne (2004, 1st published 1952) *Witchcraft*. Sutton.

Hutton, Ronald (2018) *The Witch: A History of Fear from Ancient Times to the Present*. Yale University Press.

Hutton, Ronald (1999) *The Triumph of the Moon: A History of Modern Pagan Witchcraft*. Oxford University Press.

Kramer, Heinrich & Sprenger, James (1971, 1st published 1486) *The Malleus Maleficarum*. Dover.

Lewis, James R. (1999) *Witchcraft Today: An Encyclopedia of Wiccan and Neopagan Traditions*. ABC-Clio.

Lewis, James R. and Rabinovitch, Shelley (2002). *The Encyclopedia of Modern Witchcraft and Neo-Paganism*. Citadel Press.

Masello, Robert (1996) *Raising Hell: A Concise History of the Black Arts – and Those Who Dared to Practice Them*. Penguin Putnam.

Maxwell-Stuart, P. G. (2006). *Witch Hunters*. Tempus.

Maxwell – Stuart, P. G. (2004) *Witchcraft: A History*. Tempus.

Maxwell – Stuart, P. G. (2004) *Wizards: A History*. Tempus.

Medway, Gareth J. (2001) *Lure of the Sinister: The Unnatural History of Satanism*. New York University Press.

Nathan, Debbie (1995) *Satan's Silence: Ritual Abuse and the Making of a Modern American Witch Hunt*. Basic Books.

Russell, Jeffrey Burton (2007) *A New History of Witchcraft: Sorcerers, Heretics, and Pagans*. Thames and Hudson.

Scott, Reginald (1972, 1st published 1584) *The Discoverie of Witchcraft*. Dover.

Timbers, Frances (2019) *A History of Magic and Witchcraft: Sabbats, Satan, and Superstitions in the West*. Pen and Sword.

Victor, Jeffery S. (1993) *Satanic Panic: The Creation of a Contemporary Legend*. Open Court.

Chapter 9. Contemporary Satanism – Followers and Admirers of the Devil Today

The belief that hidden among the respectable are groups who worship and revere the Devil and regard him as their God, has been around for almost as long as the monotheistic faiths themselves. A frequent feature of Christian and Muslim polemic has been to accuse various groups of being Satanists, inspired by the Devil and following him. These accusations are completely baseless and reflect a recurring fantasy, which has sparked off a series of moral panics historically, including the ones discussed in Chapter 8. Alternatively, they either reflect the idea that anything opposed to the Church is by definition Satanic or they are cynical and done with the intent of discrediting other ideas by association. However, in the twentieth century the revaluation of Satan that had begun in literature over a hundred years earlier bears fruit in the shape of actual real-life Satanists and real, organised Satanism. This is now a new religious movement, small but organised and active.

From the earliest days of the Church we find the idea that any form of religion other than Christianity is a form of Devil worship, with pagan gods categorised as demons (as described in Chapter7). Later, as the arguments over points of doctrine and the definition of key concepts such as the Trinity and the two natures of Jesus became intense, charges of being a follower of Satan were typically levelled at heretics (those who persisted in disagreeing with the official doctrine of the Church). Later on, the popular idea of Muslims as found in works such as Chansons de Geste was that they were Devil worshippers. Obviously, in a Christian society the charge of being a follower and worshipper of the Enemy was the most serious that could possibly be made. It was used most spectacularly in the case of the Knights Templar during the suppression of the Order by Phillip IV of France between 1307 and 1312. In that instance the charge was that the Templars were secretly worshippers of Satan in the form of Baphomet. According to the confessions of the knights (extracted under torture and so unreliable to say the least), this was a head, possibly with three faces. They were also supposed to have blasphemed and denied the truth of Christianity with rituals such as spitting on the Cross.

In the eighteenth century and the Age of Reason, scepticism about Christianity in particular (as opposed to religion in general) became popular among some elite circles. One form that this took were secret societies that propagated ideas that were still dangerous to express publicly, even for members of the upper classes (or maybe particularly for them, because of the political implications of people in their positions having such ideas). The best-known case of this was Freemasonry, particularly on the Continent but also in the UK. More dramatic were the underground sex clubs such as the Beggars Benison society and the Hellfire Clubs discussed in Chapter 5. Here the evidence that there was actual blasphemous ritual involved is strong. However, there is no evidence that Dashwood and the others who met at Medmenham actually believed in the Devil.

What did happen though was that for conservatives and particularly conservative Catholics the French Revolution and its aftermath were seen as an eruption of the demonic and Satanic into an orderly Christian world. This found its classic expression in the writings of the Abbe Augustin Barruel, particularly his massive work of 1798-99 *Memoirs Illustrating the History of Jacobinism*, in which he argued that the Revolution was the product of a conspiracy inspired by Freemasons and followers of the occult (which he conflated). Similar arguments were made independently by his British counterpart John Robison in his *Proofs of a Conspiracy against all the Religions and Governments of Europe, carried on in the secret meetings of Freemasons, Illuminati and Reading Societies* from 1797. This idea was transmitted by later authors such as Nesta Webster and William Guy Carr and is still found in some circles today (although the descendants of alien lizards now often take the place formerly occupied by demons).

Throughout the nineteenth century the belief that there was a vast revolutionary conspiracy, associated with Freemasonry but ultimately inspired by occultism or even outright worship of the Devil (usually called 'Luciferianism') was a commonplace of reactionary Catholic thought. This was particularly the case in France for various reasons and there were a number of serious panics or hysterias about this subject there as late as the 1890s. At the same time however, there was a cultural movement that actually did involve the occult and even parodic Satanism, in the shape of the nineteenth century occult revival. This was a complex and multifaceted movement with a number of different sources and expressions, including the revival and reconstruction of old pre-Christian pagan religions, but these do not concern us here. What does was an aspect of the revival that happened mainly in France. Its central figure was the occultist and scholar Eliphas Levi. Levi (real name Alphonse Louis Constant) was a sometime socialist and radical who became a student and scholar of Western esotericism or hermeticism. Between 1850 and his death in 1875 he published a series of studies of ritual magic, such as the *History of Magic* (1860), and *Transcendental Magic, Its Doctrine and Ritual* (1854-6).

What Levi did was to effectively create the modern form of magical occultism. He was responsible for several of its main features, such as the incorporation of Jewish mysticism or Kabbalah, in the shape of Tarot cards. He also set out several of its key ideas, such as the importance of will and the idea that the essence of magic was to bring about effects in the material world through mental effort. He was also responsible for creating several of the main icons or images of modern occultism. One of these was the Baphomet. He took the name given to the head supposedly venerated by the Templars and applied it to a representation of the Devil often found in Medieval art, particularly statuary, in which Satan is represented as a seated figure with a human torso and a goat's legs and head with horns, with one hand pointing up and the other down. Levi added some details of his own, such as breasts, because the figure was meant to represent the union of opposites. This has gone on the become perhaps the best-known symbol of contemporary occultism and Satanism. Levi himself was not a practitioner of ritual magic and his only attempt to perform a ritual ended in near disaster. However, he inspired a succession of subsequent figures and, along with other figures such as the English politician and author Edward Bulwer-Lytton, effectively began a modern movement of magic and the occult. Levi was not himself a Satanist or follower of the Devil but a central aspect of his thought was the idea that the dark side of the universe was not something radically opposed to the other, good side but part of a united and harmonious whole. That meant rejection of the classical Christian conception of the Devil and an attitude towards him that was much more open or welcoming.

Among later figures strongly influenced by Levi were well known people such as Madame Blavatsky, the founder of Theosophy, as well as a whole cluster of people who together formed what we may call an occult underground in the France of the 1890s. Among the leading figures were Stanislas de Guaita, Josephin Peladan, the Abbe Joseph – Antoine Boullan, and Papus (real name Gerard Encausse). The novelist Joris-Karl Huysmans was a member of this group for a while and described some of its practices and internal feuds in his writings, particularly the novel *La Bas* (1891). De Guaita adapted the figure of Baphomet to create the goat pentagram, in which a goat's head appears inside an inverted pentagram – this went on to become the definitive symbol of organised Satanism. (It appeared in his work *La Clef de la Magie Noire,* published in 1897). However, for our purposes his major effect was in the United Kingdom at around the same time.

The event here was the founding in 1887 of the Hermetic Order of the Golden Dawn, by William Robert Woodman, William Wynn Westcott, and Samuel Liddell McGregor Mathers. The Golden Dawn was a secret society devoted to the study and practice of esoteric knowledge and ritual magic. All three of its founders were masons and (more significantly) had a keen interest in the systematic ideas put forward by Levi in his various books. The Golden Dawn came to have many well-known and prominent people among its members such as Sir Arthur Conan Doyle, William Butler Yeats, and the Irish revolutionary Maud Gonne. It also included people who would play a major part in twentieth century literature of horror and the occult such as Arthur Machen and Algernon Blackwood. Most important for subsequent developments were two members: A. E. Waite and the self-styled 'wickedest man in the world', Aleister Crowley. It was Waite who translated a number of classic works of occultism into English and also created the edition of the tarot deck that most people know today. It was Crowley however who would have the biggest impact.

Crowley did not remain a member of the Golden Dawn for long, having a spectacular falling out with McGregor Mathers. However, he went on the become the most notorious and infamous occultist of the twentieth century. In the early 1900s he founded his own religion, Thelema. The word, which is Greek in origin means 'will' and the central principle of its thought is *"Do What Thou Wilt Shall Be The Whole of the Law"*. This principle, which in this formulation derives from the sixteenth century French author Francois Rabelais, is an assertion not only of radical individualism and rejection of the constraints of conventional morality but also of a metaphysics in which it is will (the active aspect of the mind) that creates reality for the individual. Crowley's career and the controversies he was engaged in have produced enough books and commentaries to fill several large bookcases. For our purposes the main interest is that he gave firm form to an organised movement of Left-Hand Path magic and occultism.

In the system of kabbalistic and hermetic ritual magic that was systematised by Levi there are two different kinds of magical practice and discipline, the right and left hand paths. The distinction between the two is not the same as that between white and black magic (which derives from the uses to which the exercise of magic is put). Rather they are two contrasting routes to the same end, which is self-mastery and liberation. The right-hand path is associated with self-denial, sacrifice, and the following of ethical codes while the left-hand path goes with self-assertion, physical practices such as sex magic, and the deliberate flouting of convention and moral codes. The point of course is that for someone within the Christian or Islamic tradition or a society based on one of those traditions, the left-hand path is obviously associated with the Devil. This is especially the case in the modern world, when the understanding of Satan has come to see him as the great rebel against authority and the exemplar of the assertion of individual judgment and desire against convention and obedience. So followers of the left hand path, even if not overtly or straightforwardly Satanists, will be sympathetic to him or will find the concept of image of the Christian and Islamic Devil one that they can employ, as an ideal and a way of contrasting their own position to that of conventional morality and Christianity and also forms of mysticism that derive from orthodox monotheism.

Crowley set up several organisations during his lifetime, the most significant of which was the Ordo Templi Orientalis (OTO). This had a number of followers and disciples in various parts of the world, including North America. A leading figure in that part of the world initially was an English expatriate called Wilfred Talbot Smith. In 1935 he set up a branch of the OTO in Pasadena, California which soon attracted a number of members. One of these was a truly remarkable figure called Jack Parsons. He was one of the founders of the famous Jet Propulsion Laboratory in Pasadena and was the main person behind the development of the solid fuel rocket motor. He was also deeply interested in the occult. He was charismatic and a natural leader and proselytiser for the ideas. He soon replaced Smith as the head of the branch of the

OTO and his house became the locale for a variegated collection of fellow employees at the JPL, artists and musicians and occultists.

It was also the scene of some truly extraordinary sexual goings on because of the principles the organisation followed, which included open sexual relations. Parsons was married to one woman, Helen Northrup, but then had a relationship with her younger sister Sara. Sara in turn went on to establish a relationship with L Ron Hubbard, who at this point had not yet founded Scientology (he was still developing Dianetics). Parsons for his part became obsessed with the idea of performing a magic ritual to manifest an incarnation of the Thelemic goddess Babalon. He did this in 1946 and decided that a woman he met soon afterwards called Marjorie Cameron was that incarnation. Unfortunately, Hubbard and Sara in the meantime defrauded him and even more unfortunately for him, in 1952 he was killed in a massive explosion at his house. However, his legacy was that an underground subculture of magic and the occult became established in California and later on fed into the wilder parts of the 1960s counterculture.

In that counterculture magic and an interest in the occult was one of its main features, along with rock music, experimenting with drugs, and Maoist politics. All kinds of fringe ideas suddenly began to circulate both on and off the university campuses that were the epicentre of this 'new age'. California was not the only place where this was happening of course but it was the hub. One book that played a very important part in this was *The Morning of the Magicians*, originally published in French in 1960 and written by two French journalists, louis Pauwels and Jacques Bergier. The book was a compendium of a whole range of fringe ideas such as Nazi occultism (and ideas such as the Horbiger 'Ice World cosmology), ancient astronaut theory and the supposed influence of UFOs, conspiracy theories, ritual magic and Satanism. It was translated into English and published in the United States in 1964 and became a best-seller. What it did was to make the kinds of ideas that had been circulating among groups like the one Parsons had created much more widely available and accessible. It also connected them to other fringe ideas, with the result that people interested in, for example, oriental mind disciplines or conspiracy theories would now be brought into contact with other notions such as ritual and Thelemic magick and its derivations. (This is a case of the operation of the 'cultic milieu' mentioned below). What it also did was to create a relatively large market for those ideas and this provided an entrepreneurial opportunity for people who were already part of the occult scene, particularly in California.

Someone who was a part of this subculture that Parsons had created was a man called Anton LaVey, who lived for most of his life in San Francisco, although he was born in 1930 in Chicago. LaVey told many stories about his life, such as that he worked in a circus or that subsequently, he was a photographer for the San Francisco Police Department, that turn out on examination to have no evidence for them. As a result, constructing an accurate biography is extremely difficult. What is undoubtedly true is that by the later 1950s and early 1960s he was a well-known figure in California's occult scene. He gave both formal lectures on occultism, and parties that were attended by a wide range of people from many different walks of life but united in an interest in the weird and occult. Among the people involved were Baroness Carin de Plessen, Cecil Nixon, the journalist and author Shana Alexander, Michael Harner (an anthropologist who would go on to be the major advocate of the revival of shamanism as a religious practice), and the underground film maker Kenneth Anger. Anger was a key member of the circle, not least because of his earlier connections with the Crowleyan occult scene in Southern California. He in turn would have connections with several significant people in the music business, including Mick Jagger (who was both amused and baffled by him) and Jimmy Page. The other major group in LaVey's circle was authors of science fiction and weird tales with an interest in myth and the occult, including Clark Ashton Smith, Fritz Leiber, Anthony Boucher, and August Derleth who was as responsible as anyone for the creation of the popular phenomenon of the Cthulhu Mythos based on the writings of HP Lovecraft.

On April 30th 1966 (Walpurgisnacht) LaVey formally transformed this informal network into an organisation, the Church of Satan. Unlike previous occult organisations such as the OTO or the Golden Dawn, which were initiatory study and training organisations, the Church of Satan was organised as a religion, with LaVey as its head. It was also not simply a hermetic or esoteric organisation in terms of its doctrine. Instead it combined a number of elements, including ones from occultism, to produce something novel. One of these was to explicitly define itself as a Satanist movement that venerated Satan. What he created was one of the many New Religious Movements that sprang up at this time. It has shown staying power, surviving his death and a split with his daughter

Karla (who has set up her own organisation). The Church of Satan is still very much a going concern and LaVeyan Satanism as it is now known, is the most widespread form of contemporary Satanism. LaVey himself ran the CoS until his death in 1997 after which that role was taken over by his partner Blanche Barton. She in turn stepped down in 2001 and handed over control to Peter Gilmore and Peggy Nadramia, who continue to run it, having moved its headquarters from San Francisco to Hell's Kitchen, New York. Anton LaVey's older daughter Karla was a prominent figure until she left to set up her own organisation, the First Satanic Church in San Francisco, which claims to continue the tradition of her father. Her younger sister Zeena was the High Priestess and public face of the CoS in the 1980s but she then became estranged from her family and converted to Buddhism.

In the later 1960s and early 1970s LaVey produced a series of books that developed and spelt out this doctrine, starting with *The Satanic Bible* in 1969. All of these are still in print, and selling well. There are also sequels or supplements produced by figures such as LaVey's successors, Blanche Barton and Peter Gilmore. The doctrine is also set out via the Church of Satan's website and those of its followers (which tend to spring up and vanish like mushrooms), all of which set out the same basic perspective. This is a combination of three elements or sources. The first is the ideas of modern occultism, as developed in the nineteenth and twentieth centuries in the way described earlier. There was also an influence from the ideas and style of the later nineteenth century Decadent movement, not directly but as mediated through science fiction and fantasy (particularly of the macabre or weird variety) and through the world of the circus or carnival, which LaVey knew directly. The second is a species of egoistic individualism that can be traced back to Nietzsche, particularly as presented by the American author E L Mencken. One text from that tradition that was clearly a source was the 1896 work *Might is Right* by 'Ragnar Redbeard' (a pseudonym that is commonly believed to have been used by the New Zealand author Arthur Desmond). We can tell this because large parts of the *Satanic Bible* are paraphrases of the older work. The websites of the Church of Satan and its followers regularly recommend the work, along with the writings of Nietzsche and the American novelist/philosopher Ayn Rand (a contemporary of LaVey's although there is no evidence of their knowing each other – there is only the shared ethical egoism). The third is modern self-help literature and in particular the tradition of New Thought, a widespread feature of American popular culture from the 1890s onwards. The central idea of this tradition is that thoughts and attitudes can affect or shape the material world and events, hence the notion of success due to 'positive thinking' or 'positive mental attitude'.

The main feature of LaVeyan Satanism as a system of thought is perhaps a surprising one. Satan or the Devil is not believed to actually exist or be a person or entity, whether physical or spiritual. Instead, the word Satan is used to refer to an idea or image that has powerful motivating qualities for the practitioner and provides a focus for a particular way of thinking, feeling and living. In one sense Satan is an idealised model of how people should be. The essence of this is a complete rejection of Christianity, not only in its metaphysical aspects but in its ethics. LaVeyan Satanists are therefore atheists and materialists who totally reject Christian ethics and advocate instead what Nietzsche called a 'transvaluation of values'. This means a reversal of conventional moral standards as found in Christianity or derived from it, in which the conventional Christian virtues become blameworthy and the traditional sins virtues and qualities to admire and emulate. Meekness is despised, power and mastery are elevated, lust is celebrated and hedonism is thought better than self-denial. This can take the form of a predatory egoism but in most of the works there are strong warnings against this since preying on others is another form of dependency. The focus is rather on self-sufficiency, self-direction and personal discipline, and enjoyment of the physical world. There is also a definite elitism and contempt for the 'common herd'. Atheistic Satanism of this kind therefore combines atheism and rejection of existing religions (particularly Christianity) with individualism and ethical egoism, hedonism, elitism, and philosophical materialism. What it does is to take many of the qualities traditionally ascribed to the Devil and to redefine them as virtues. It also takes one of the modern images or conceptions of the Devil, which sees him as a heroic and self-asserting autonomous rebel, and makes that an ideal while detaching that ideal from the belief in an actual entity.

Alongside this mixture of ethical philosophy and pop psychology is a great deal of what we may call practical lifestyle advice of the kind commonly found in self-help literature, such as the need for affirmation and mental rituals. The teaching of the Church of Satan as regards lifestyle and ethics is summed up in the three lists "The Nine Satanic Statements", "The Eleven Satanic Rules of the Earth", and "The Nine Satanic Sins". The first is a series of affirmations such as "Satan represents indulgence instead of abstinence!", "Satan represents vital existence instead of spiritual pipe dreams!" and "Satan represents vengeance instead of turning the other cheek!" while the sins are stupidity, pretentiousness, solipsism, self-deceit, herd conformity, lack of perspective, forgetfulness of past orthodoxies, counterproductive pride, and lack of aesthetics. If he were still with us LaVey would no doubt be both disgusted and amused by the prevalence of these today. The "Rules of the earth" are a series of commandments with striking similarities to the Laws of the Jungle in Kipling's Jungle Book – the message (also found in the Statements) is that human beings are animals by nature but should accept that rather than trying to deny it. The texts can be found by following the link in the 'Further Reading".

This is combined with a particular idea of magic, which LaVey seems to have worked out himself but which is similar to the ideas found in the works of other twentieth century occultists, such as Crowley and the Russian/French author Maria de Naglowska. This is firstly that magic as an activity and practice is about the will and about deliberately evoking and creating certain states of mind in oneself or others through rituals and various practices, with those states of mind then consciously controlled and directed. The second is that magic exists at two levels. The first, quotidian or common, level consists of what is basically psychological manipulation to create effects that appear magical to bystanders or those affected but which are in fact natural. The point is that this is presented as being a conscious and deliberate skill or technique that can be learned and perfected (which indeed it is in many ways). This is called 'magic' but it is actually the skills or practice of the grifter or pick-up artist generalized and systematized. The second kind or level of magic is the higher one. Here rituals and mental techniques are combined to actually bring about changes in the physical world and course of events in accordance with the will – the classic modern definition of systematic magic. LaVey firmly asserts that this can happen but qualifies this by saying that this is difficult and not to be undertaken lightly or casually.

The Church of Satan has produced a number of offshoots or breakaways over the years. Many of these are simply rival versions of the same basic ideas and practice with the only real division being one of personalities. There is one though that is a distinct and different movement. This is the temple of Set, and the associated religion of Setianism. This was founded in 1975 by a remarkable if bizarre character called Michael Aquino. He came from a background in military intelligence before joining the Church of Satan soon after it was founded and becoming one of its leading members. He split with LaVey in 1975 and then (by his own account) invoked and successfully raised Satan in a ritual. Satan told him that he should be called Set, the name used for him in the ancient Egyptian religion and gave him a revelation and mission. Aquino and several others who had followed him out of the Church of Satan then set up the Temple of Set. Unlike LaVeyan Satanism, this is a form of theistic Satanism in which Satan is thought to be an actual being who is worthy of worship. The basic Biblical story is kept but with the evaluations reversed so that the Fall becomes a liberation in which the Devil (Set) gives humanity the gift of reason and a questioning intellect (the so-called 'Black Flame'). As well as being theistic as opposed to atheistic the Temple of Set differs from the Church of Satan in another important respect. Whereas the CoS has an organisation similar to that of a self-help group, the Temple of Set is more like a traditional initiatory and ritual based organisation. The main activity is a disciplined and structured one of acquiring greater knowledge and capacity by progression through a series of stages, in a way that is familiar from other secret societies and mystery religions.

The Temple of Set is not the only variety of theistic Satanism out there. There are in fact many exponents of that variety to be found on the internet or in parts of the counterculture. This kind of Satanism typically is less of a guide on how to live (in the way that LaVeyan Satanism is) and much more associated with regular modern occultism and the practice of ritual magic. A strong influence in the last two to three decades has been 'chaos magic'. This is a theory and practice of magic that is self-consciously eclectic. The idea is that the practitioner can use any kind of mythological or even made up system of beliefs and mythology – the only question is does it work for them? The result is people drawing on all kinds of mythical systems including some such as the Cthulhu Mythos of H P Lovecraft (or more properly August Derleth) that derive from popular weird fiction. One obvious choice is to use the mythological figure of the Devil, hence the increasing number of theistic Satanists. They are not organized or structured in the way that the Temple of Set and Church of Satan are, but there is an underground world of temporary organisations, publishers, and individuals in which certain figures are particularly prominent and influential. The two most important are Michael Ford, and Stephanie Connolly, both of whom are prolific authors with an active online presence.

Alongside overtly and explicitly Satanist organisations and individuals in the contemporary world are people and bodies that are part of the modern occult tradition without being full-on supporters of Satan as either an actual entity or an ideal. These are cases where although the figure of Satan is not venerated or worshipped, he is still not regarded in the way that he is in the traditional Christian or Islamic account of him. For some, mostly neopagan movements he is either ignored completely, as a part of the monotheistic belief system that they reject, or he is seen as simply a traditional dark god of the kind found in most polytheistic systems and therefore not as the malevolent adversary. For others he is a more benign figure, not perhaps the central one but a part of a larger system of ideas in which he and the ideas associated with him are viewed in an ambivalent or positive light without him becoming the central figure. The main examples of this are various movements and individuals that carry on the Thelemic tradition put together by Crowley earlier on in the twentieth century, and this tradition, which things like LaVeyan Satanism grew out of, are still very much with us.

One thing worth noting is the common connection between Satanism and certain kinds of politics. This takes two very different forms. There is a recurring connection with certain kinds of fascist or far right politics, particularly the stranger forms of esoteric Naziism or the kinds of far right thought and activism influenced by the Italian thinker Julius Evola. There is a strong historic precedent for this in a way because of the connection between far-right politics in the Germanic parts of Europe and esoteric neo-paganism, which was a feature of fin de siècle Vienna among other places and had a continuing influence on certain figures in the leadership of the Third Reich, most notably Heinrich Himmler. This however was not directly connected to any kind of explicit Satanism despite some wild and entertaining conspiracy theories. Since 1945 however there have been such connections and this became noticeable during the 1990s in particular. However, the majority of contemporary Satanists disavow that kind of politics, even though there is an obvious fit with the elitism. Instead there is often a leaning towards a form of individualist politics and a species of libertarianism, very different to the first kind of orientation.

Contemporary Satanism is not mainstream by any stretch of the imagination but it has been more successful than one might expect. Given that its central position, viewing the historical figure of the Devil in a positive light, involves rejecting most of the intellectual and cultural history of Western civilisation and inverting its moral code to a great degree, it is not surprising that it remains a fringe belief. What is surprising is just how widespread it is as a fringe movement. There are no accurate figures but academic studies show that there are Satanists in all places and walks of life. There is a definite subculture and social network as well as the stereotypical isolated teenagers. What Anton LaVey did was to create a particular subculture or counterculture that has proved to be self-perpetuating and capable of further growth and development. At present the various varieties of Satanism exist within what the British sociologist Colin Campbell called the 'cultic milieu', the underworld of fringe and marginalised beliefs and ideas that mingle and rub up against one another, at one time in obscure bookshops and clubs, now more often in various parts of cyberspace. As in essence a combination of radical elitist individualism and antichristian ethics there is a definite constituency for it. What is striking is how distinct and separate it has remained on the whole from other movements found in that milieu (one of its features is that people who start off with one fringe idea or belief borrow others from other people they meet, in a circulation and cross-pollination of dissident notions). The reasons for this would seem to be firstly its definite rationalism and scepticism (opposition to faith being one of its main elements) and secondly its sociological basis. In any event we have now arrived at the point where the Devil has people who explicitly count themselves as fans and supporters, of at least the image and idea, sometimes of the actual person. Things have definitely moved in a novel direction.

Further Reading
Barton, Blanche (1992) *The Secret Life of a Satanist: The Authorized Biography of Anton LaVey*. Feral House.

Barton, Blanche (1990) *The Church of Satan*. Hell's Kitchen Productions.

Carter, John (1999) *Sex and Rockets: The Occult World of Jack Parsons*. Feral House.

Cavendish, Richard. (1967) *The Black Arts*. Penguin Putnam.

Connolly, Stephanie (2006) *The Complete Book of Demonolatry*. DB Publishing.

Coughlin, John J. (1997) *Out of the Shadows: An Exploration of Dark Paganism and Magick*. 1st Books.

Drury, Nevill (2000) *The History of Magic in the Modern Age: A Quest for Personal Transformation*. Constable.

DuQuette, Lon Milo (2003): *The Magick of Aleister Crowley: A Handbook of the Rituals of Thelema*, Weiser Books.

Dyrendal, Asbjorn, Lewis, James R., Petersen, Jesper AA. (2016) *The Invention of Modern Satanism*. Oxford University Press.

Faxneld, Per and Petersen, Jesper AA. (2012). *The Devil's Party: Satanism in Modernity*. Oxford University Press.

Ford, Michael W. (2005) *Luciferian Witchcraft*. Succubus Publishing.

Gilmore, Peter H. (2007) *The Satanic Scriptures*. Scapegoat Publishing.

Introvigne, Massimo (2016). *Satanism: A Social History*. Brill.

LaVey, Anton Szandor (1992) *The Satanic Bible*. Feral House.

LaVey, Anton Szandor (1998) *The Satanic Rituals*. Feral House.

LaVey, Anton Szandor (1998) *Satan Speaks!* Feral House.

LaVey, Anton Szandor (1992) *The Devil's Notebook*. Feral House.

LaVey, Anton Szandor (1989, 1st published 1970) *The Satanic Witch*. Feral House.

Levi, Eliphas (2006) *Magic: A History of its Rites, Rituals, and Mysteries*. Dover.

Levi, Eliphas (2019) *Transcendental Magic: Its Doctrine and Ritual*. Yesterday's World Publishing.

Lewis, James R. (2001) *Satanism Today: An Encyclopedia of Religion, Folklore, and Popular Culture.* ABC – Clio.

Pauwels, Louis & Bergier, Jacques (2001, 1st published 1960) *The Morning of the Magicians.* Souvenir Press.

Petersen, Jesper Agaard (ed.) (2009) *Contemporary Religious Satanism: A Critical Anthology.* Ashgate.

Tucker, Robert C. (1999) *An Age For Lucifer: Predatory Spirituality and The Quest For Godhood.* Holmes Publishing Group.

Webb, James (1988 1st pub. 1974) *The Occult Underground.* Open Court.

Weir, David (2018) *Decadence: A Very Short Introduction.* Oxford University Press. https://www.churchofsatan.com/theory-practice/

Chapter 10. The Devil in Art and Literature

The Devil as a subject has attracted many of the greatest writers and artists. He has inspired and figured prominently in many great works as well as in some truly terrible ones (maybe even deserving the epithet 'diabolical'). The reason why so many writers great and not so great have written about him or had him figure in their works is simple: he is a fascinating character, beguiling yet terrible, and by his nature can be used to give insight into the darker side of human nature and the human condition. Moreover, the figure of the Devil can be used to great effect in skilful hands to satirise and mock the existing state of affairs and conventional pieties. The hypocrisy of everyday life and also of affairs of state offers great opportunities for this. There are several of the great works of Western and world literature and art in which Satan plays a major or central part. The differences in the ways that they portray him and in the part he plays in the story reveal changes in the way the Devil is understood or thought of and in the concerns and anxieties of the authors and of society in general in their times (to the extent that they are representative). On the other hand, the greatest works, such as those of Milton or Dante, also have an impact on the way the culture at large conceives of the Devil, so they shape and influence the ideas as well as reflecting them.

During the Middle Ages Satan appears mainly in the vision narratives of Hell that we looked at in Chapter 6, and in works of popular drama such as morality and mystery plays. In the latter he was often a figure of fun tending to the burlesque, grotesque and repulsive but not terrible, reflecting medieval emphases on his physical nature and defeated state. The writer who both concluded the Medieval portrayal of the Devil and at the same time transcended it and opened the way to new ways of envisaging him was Dante. His great work was the *Divine Comedy*, a poem of ninety-nine cantos in which Dante himself undertakes a journey through each of the realms of Hell (the *Inferno*), Purgatory (the *Purgatorio*), and Heaven (the *Paradiso*). His guide through Hell and Purgatory is the Roman poet Virgil. The Devil himself does not appear in the Inferno until the thirty fourth canto where Dante suddenly sees him as he enters the very centre of Hell. Satan is described as a giant, plunged up to the waist in the frozen lake of Cocytus where traitors of all kinds are punished. He has three faces, one red, one yellow, and one black, and six bat like wings. These beat constantly and generate an icy wind that freezes the lake around him. In each of his three mouths he gnaws on one of the three arch traitors to their lords (the worst of all sins for Dante), Brutus, Cassius, and Judas Iscariot (who also has his back flayed constantly by the Devil's claws). As he chews on them, he weeps bloody tears that run down his faces and mingle with the slaver that drips from his chins.

Satan in Dante's portrayal is utterly physical. This can be seen in the detailed account of his physical appearance and of the punishment and suffering of the three arch-sinners. He is bestial and grotesque – at the end of the canto as Vergil and Dante climb down his thighs and then up his legs (having passed the centre of gravity at the middle of the Earth) we are told that he is covered in coarse hair. His features reflect his nature – as a former angel of the order of the seraphim he has six wings but because of his fall they are now dark and bat-like. Where once he was beautiful, he is now monstrous and ugly. His threefold head is a blasphemous reflection of the Trinity and the triune nature of God (and also arguably reflects his rule until the Resurrection over the three races of humanity). Above all he is helpless and defeated. Having rebelled and tried to supplant God he is now totally imprisoned, unable to do anything except weep tears of rage and despair and mangle the three in his jaws. The genius of Dante makes the description both terrifying and repulsive yet at the same time pathetic. This image of the Devil, which drew on and, in a sense, perfected earlier ones, fixed the physical image of Satan for contemporaries and at the same time allowed later writers to move on from it.

The evolving image of the Devil in literature after Dante reflects the way conceptions of him and his nature changed during the Renaissance and Reformation. He becomes, as we have seen, more powerful and less physical. At the same time the stories and accounts associated with the great witch hunts still give him a physical reality, as can be seen by their accounts of initial meetings with him. A crucial change is that he becomes less grotesque and more beguiling, yet in some ways more sinister. This is captured in the portrayal of Mephistopheles (supposedly a lesser fallen angel but representative of the Devil) in Marlowe's *Doctor Faustus*. He is not the terrible but helpless and imprisoned Satan of Dante but rather supple, helpful, inveigling, and subtle. However, the work that definitely changed the way Satan was represented and has probably had more influence in that regard than any other text over the last few hundred years was written in England in the middle of the seventeenth century. That is of course Milton's *Paradise Lost*.

Paradise Lost is often considered the greatest poem in the English language. It is certainly one of the longest, and the grandest in scope. It starts halfway through the story, with Satan and his cohorts finding themselves plunged into the fiery lake of Hell after being defeated and cast out of Heaven and falling through space for nine days. Later, in book five of the poem, the Archangel Rafael tells Adam the story of how Satan led a rebellion in heaven before the world was created and subverted many of his fellow angels to his cause. He is then defeated through the intervention of the Son and cast out of heaven with his cohorts. The main focus of the poem however is the temptation of Adam and Eve by the Devil and their Fall and expulsion from Eden. Milton's organisation of the work in this way serves a dramatic purpose. It presents the reader with the central character, Satan, in the aftermath of defeat, and enables the poet to fix an image of him that is one of the most powerful in English literature, before going on to recount both the prequel and the sequel.

One key to understanding the dynamics of the poem and the way in which the Devil is portrayed in it is that Satan is the central character in the epic. Above all he is the active character, it is his actions and character that drive the story and lead to its events and outcome. As such he occupies the role of the hero in most epics but he is of course the anti-hero, the embodiment of evil and malice rather than virtue. In order for the effect to work however he has to have apparent agency and ability to act – he cannot be a helpless prisoner like Dante's Lucifer. He also has to have qualities that are normally associated with the hero or central figure of the hero narrative such as courage, indomitability, and defiance. In the story Satan has the quality of the sublime – this means that he evokes feelings of both awe and terror. He is charismatic, given great flights of expansive rhetoric by Milton, he refuses to accept defeat and is clearly the leader of his fellows, who inspires the initial revolt and bolsters their courage after their defeat.

All this can be seen in various key points in the narrative. Initially there is Satan's great speech of defiance, in which he rejects the idea and even the possibility of repentance, concluding with the famous lines "*to reign is worth ambition though in Hell, better to reign in Hell than serve in Heaven*". Later he undertakes a perilous journey to gain access to the newly created Earth so that he can carry out his plot of revenging himself on God by subverting Adam and Eve. In the course of this he has an introspective soliloquy in which he considers the hopelessness of his position but resolves to press in his hostility to God. He is in some ways a heroic figure, in the traditional understanding of that identity and Milton certainly gives him all of the best lines.

At the same time however, Milton clearly tells the reader that this is a matter of appearance rather than reality. Satan is solipsistic and self-absorbed, a quality captured right at the start in the initial speech with the well-known lines "*Farewell, happy fields, Where joy for ever dwells! Hail, horrors! hail, Infernal world! and thou, profoundest Hell, Receive thy new possessor – one who brings A mind not to be changed by place or time. The mind is its own place, and in itself Can make a Heaven of Hell, a Hell of Heaven. What matter where, if I be still the same*". There is here a wilful assertion of the complete independence and autonomy of the individual mind and denial of reality. It is also clear that he is the embodiment of spite, resentment, and malice as in the lines from Book III "*Farewell remorse; all good to me is lost. Evil, be thou my good.*" and from Book I "*To do aught good, never will be our task, But ever to do ill, our sole delight, As being the contrary to His high will, Whom we resist*". But the most fundamental point is that ultimately Satan does not have agency and in some ways is not the protagonist of the story because no matter what he does it will serve God's purpose and is all part of His plan. Satan simply doesn't get it – he does not realise that God is God, that he is omniscient and omnipotent; or more to the point he refuses to accept it because of his pride and narcissism. The Fall is actually part of God's purpose because it makes possible a higher form of virtue, in fact the greatest possible in the shape of the redemptive death and resurrection of Jesus. (The modern critic William Empson argued that this means that God is not innocent with regard to the wickedness of Satan's scheme and the suffering it brings about).

However, one of the realities of texts and reading is that readers can create their own meaning for the text, independent of any purpose that the author may have had. *Paradise Lost* is the great illustration of this point. As the seventeenth century passed and the eighteenth and subsequent centuries followed, the way that Milton meant the figure of Satan to be understood was not the way many readers responded to the text – perhaps because so many of them, like Satan, no longer believed in a God with the qualities of omniscience and omnipotence. The figure of Satan as portrayed by Milton is often seen as truly heroic, even admirable and inspiring. His attack on the hypocrisy of God in the speeches that inspire one third of his fellows to rebel with him is seen as right on target by authors of whom Philip Pullman is only the latest example. William Blake, who saw Satan as a heroic figure, famously observed that *"The reason Milton wrote in fetters when he wrote of Angels & God, and at liberty when of Devils & Hell, is because he was a true Poet and of the Devil's party without knowing it"*. Blake's view has been widespread and most Romantics have, like him, leaned towards Satan.

Essentially in the world since Milton wrote his great poem, Satan has come to be seen by many as the great rebel, the one who defies and rejects an unjustified authority and rule. His quality of individualism and self-assertion is seen as admirable so he becomes in some sense an exemplar even if a flawed one. Adding to this reading is the way that Milton deliberately gives Satan some of the physical appearance and qualities of the classical Apollonian hero (until his transformation into a snake at the end of the poem). So, this is the starting point for both a portrayal of the devil that updates the traditional Christian understanding and also for the more modern and increasingly post-Christian one that sees him in an ambivalent or even positive light and as a figurative representation of something admirable. In the later nineteenth century this latter approach was found in movements such as Symbolism and Decadence and the writings of authors such as Baudelaire. However, there was also reassertion of both the reality of the Devil and his malign power in the world and human life.

The greatest example in literature of this last phenomenon is the novel *Brothers Karamazov*, the final and for many the greatest novel of Fyodor Dostoevsky. Dostoevsky became a devout Orthodox Christian and convinced of the malign effects of the materialism and individualism of modernity. For him the Devil is a metaphysical yet real person, who exists in the minds of humans as a real and powerful force that leads to cruelty, deception, and self-destructiveness. In *Brothers Karamazov* the overt plot concerns parricide and a series of disputes and tensions between four brothers, three of them legitimate. Geoffrey Russel has argued convincingly that one way of reading this complex book is to see the family all together as a single person, with each of the four brothers and their father representing an aspect of the typical human mind and character. The key character in the book's portrayal of the Devil is the second son Ivan, who is a materialistic and individualistic atheist intellectual. Ivan in a powerful section of the book denies the existence of God in the course of a debate he has with the youngest legitimate brother Alyosha. Ivan's argument, which leads him to the conclusion that we live in a godforsaken or godless world because his logic does not allow him any other conclusion, is based on the existence of not only suffering but deliberate, callous and malevolent evil on the part of human beings. How could a God, much less a benign one, have created or allowed this?

What follows from Ivan is a self-contained prose poem (often printed on its own) the tale of the Grand Inquisitor. The story is that Jesus returns, to sixteenth century Seville. He is arrested by the Grand Inquisitor, who recognises him for what he is, but condemns him and orders him to leave and this time never return. The Inquisitor's argument is that human beings are not fit for the freedom that God has given them and will always freely chose evil and vice over virtue. The Devil, for the Inquisitor, is wise and understands this, and therefore he and the Church are doing the Devil's work. He argues that in his temptation in the wilderness Jesus should have done all of the things that the Devil urges him to do (turn stones into bread, cast himself down from the Temple but save himself, and become ruler of the world) as these were the right things to do. The Inquisitor represents earthly authorities and rulers and institutions, who (knowingly in this case) are doing the Devil's work.

Ivan though denies the Devil as he does God but as Russell puts it *"Ivan's denial of the Devil's existence is a denial of the demonic in himself, but both burst back upon him in the form of a vision or nightmare"*. (Russell, 1988: 254) The Devil appears to Ivan as a charming gentleman (the typical representation of Satan from the later nineteenth century onwards) who changes shape and appearance. Ivan recognises the Devil as an embodiment of the dark side of his nature but makes the mistake of thinking that this means he controls it himself; something the Devil encourages him to think. He does not realise that the Devil is still an independent force of malice and cruelty, even if he is also part of him and all other people. This reflects the idea found in authors as different as Baudelaire and C. S. Lewis that the Devil's smartest move has been to convince us that he does not exist. There have been other writers in the more recent past who have believed in a personal Devil and had this play a part in their work. One is the aforementioned C. S. Lewis, in his space trilogy, particularly the second volume (*Perelandra*) where the Devil makes a personal appearance. Another is the Southern American writer Flannery O'Connor. In popular fiction the major example is Tolkien, whose portrayal of the Enemy in his works (Morgoth and Sauron) reflects his conservative Catholicism.

In the twentieth century the Devil has been used in literature as a way of satirising and criticising the hypocrisy and moral failings of what we may broadly call the 'establishment', which exists to some degree in all countries. This also provides a critique of modern society and above all its rejection of the divine. The best example of this, and one of the great works of twentieth century literature is *The Master and Margerita*, by the Soviet author Mikhail Bulgakov. The book was written during Stalin's rule but only published (in a redacted form) in 1967. The 'uncut' version is now available. The novel takes place in two locations, in Moscow under atheistic Communist rule, in the elite district where most of the Soviet literary elite live (the greater part), and in Judea at the time of Christ, featuring the trial of Jesus (called Yeshua in the book) and Pontius Pilate. The Devil visits Moscow under the name of Professor Woland, along with a supernatural retinue that includes inter alia a talking black cat and a vampire. He spends his time making fun of and toying with the corrupt and cynical literary elite. While there he holds a Spring ball on Good Friday which is attended by a series of dark or evil figures from human history who are now part of his court. As part of this he persuades Margarita, the lover of the Master (an author who has killed himself in despair at his persecution by the state and the destruction of his historical novel of Pontius Pilate and the trial of Jesus) to become a witch and hostess of the ball.

In this novel the Devil is portrayed as urbane, charming, deeply cynical, amusing but at the same time sinister and creepy. The novel partly satirises the corruption, venality and cruelty of the Soviet elite and highlights their spiritual and moral emptiness. This godlessness, found elsewhere as well as in the Soviet Union, has left the world open to the principle and power of evil in the person of the Devil, who as in Dostoevsky, exists mainly inside the minds of people but is also a distinct person or entity. The novel has a comical aspect but the humour is dark and ultimately it is a deeply serious work. One of the Devil's actions in the book is to grant Margarita a wish. He expects that she will use this to serve her own wishes and so confirm her damnation. Instead she asks that one of the damned souls she met at the ball be released from her eternal punishment. On being given a second wish she asks that her lover, the Master, be resurrected so that she may live with him even if in poverty. The Devil does so but then he brings about the deaths of the Master and Margerita who join his court but are not subjected to punishment (instead they exist in a state rather like that of Limbo). This demonstrates both his essential malevolence, despite his urbane appearance, and the difficulty of virtue in the corrupted world of modernity.

As well as being a major figure in major novels and poems, the Devil has also figured prominently in modern popular fiction and related media. Thus, he appears as the central character in Mark Twain's highly disturbing posthumous story *The Mysterious Stranger*, a dark story of despair and nihilism. He is also one of the central figures in John Updike's *The Witches of Eastwick*, where his persona, Darryl Van Horne, appears at first to be a benevolently disruptive force in the lives of three women trapped in various ways by Middle American conformity but is revealed at the end as dangerous, destructive and malevolent. More recently he has figured in works such as Christopher Fowler's *Spanky* and in Clive Barker's play *The History of the Devil*. What is striking about these portrayals is that as with Bulgakov the surface of the narratives is humorous but underlying that is a profound seriousness and gravity, revealing the degree to which the Devil remains a powerful representation of and way of understanding difficult and challenging questions. He also appears frequently in comics and graphic novels, sometimes overtly, in other cases thinly disguised (many of the super-villains of the DC and Marvel universes have clearly Satanic attributes and qualities, such as the Joker for example). Perhaps the most striking recent representation of the Devil in that kind of medium is *The Sandman* by Neil Gaiman.

From its very earliest days the Devil has also figured prominently in the cinema. His portrayal in films is often wry and comical, as for example in the Peter Cook and Dudley Moore film *Bedazzled*. In other cases he is portrayed using all of the classic tropes of horror cinema, as in the film adaptation of Dennis Wheatley's *The Devil Rides Out*. This often reaches sublime levels of ridiculousness and unintended comedy and could truly deserve the epiphet of 'diabolical'. This reveals the limitations of the visual medium of film (and also television) and also the problems of portraying the Devil simply as a horrific or terrifying person in a straightforward and direct way, in a world where belief in him has lost much of its original force. Films that are more successful are ones where he remains offstage or where the presence of the Devil and his works is described using ironic and playful allusion initially and therefore hinted at rather than confronted (although in the film *Angel Heart* the name of his character Louis Cyphre is a fairly massive nudge). That film is one of the more successful, as is the film adaptation of Updike's novel. The kind of dark and nihilistic sensibility that seems to work best with film and television representations of radical evil is a common feature of much contemporary cinema, as for example in the films of Christopher Nolan.

Apart from literature, the Devil and acts in which he is involved are a frequent subject for representational art, particularly in the Medieval, Renaissance, and Baroque periods. As in literature, changes in the way the Devil is portrayed (in this case typically in the medium of painting) both reflect and cause shifts in the common understanding of his nature. The Devil is rarely the sole subject of such representations: rather he and his fellow fallen angels appear as participants in an event or as features of the representation of another related subject such as Hell. In addition to portrayals of Hell and the torments of the damned there are several other common topics that feature the Devil. These include the temptation of Adam and Eve, the rebellion of Satan and the expulsion of the fallen angels from Heaven, the Last Judgment, and the Temptation of Christ in the wilderness. There are other common subjects that are more obscure to the modern mind, in particular the Temptation of St Anthony, dealing with the efforts of the Devil to corrupt St Anthony, the founder of Christian monasticism, and other episodes from the lives of the saints. Another common topic from the later Renaissance onwards is that of witchcraft along with related topics such as that of the nightmare. This was the widespread belief in a species of demon that visited people during dreams, sitting or lying on their chests and either inspiring sexual hallucinations or actually having sex with them.

The street-wise guide to The Devil and His Works

There are certain conventions with regard to the portrayal of these events or subjects. In the case of Hell, the focus is on the torments of the damned, and their administration by demons and by Satan himself who is usually shown as bound or chained simultaneously ingesting and chewing sinners at one end while excreting them at the other. Representations of the war in Heaven and the fall of the rebel angels either show St Michael in combat with the Devil, usually shown as a dragon or serpent, being trodden under the Archangel's feet, or the actual combat between the two sides, both portrayed as winged angels but with the defeated rebels plummeting helplessly downwards and transforming as they fall from beautiful beings into hideous and monstrous ones. Paintings of the Last Judgment typically show the contrast between the joyful ascent of the blessed on the right side of the central figure of Christ in glory, and the despair and horror of the damned on his left as they fall down into Hell and are seized by demons, with Satan shown at the bottom of the scene. In the two temptations the convention is to capture the moment of temptation with the Devil as the active agent. So you have the Devil showing Jesus a stone, or holding out his hand and showing him the kingdoms of the world while in the case of Adam and Eve the Devil, often shown as a snake with limbs and the head and torso of a woman is speaking or gesturing to Eve, who either holds the Forbidden Fruit or reaches for it. Increasingly there are illustrations of particular works, most notably Dante's Inferno, where the details are determined by the actual content of the text but interpreted by the artist.

The challenge with representations of the Devil is that the Bible gives no real guidance as to how to do it, since he is never physically described, apart from his identification with the serpent in Genesis and the reference to the Devil as a dragon in Revelations. In fact, so far as we can tell there are no physical representations of him, in paintings and murals or mosaics, until the ninth century. During the Medieval period however he was portrayed frequently and an established iconography took shape very rapidly. This was derived from the traditional representation of the Greek nature god Pan and the fauns and satyrs of Greek and Roman mythology, possibly because St Jerome, one of the most prominent Christian Fathers, had described them as demons. The Devil is shown as half human, half goat with hairy goat's legs and cloven hooves. He has horns, and frequently has a flat nose and red hair. One representation, familiar now from its use in contemporary popular culture, shows him as a half human goat figure, seated cross legged and holding up one hand in a parody of blessing. His appearing in the form of a snake or dragon is less common until the Renaissance.

During the Middle Ages popular drawings or paintings of the Devil have a burlesque quality, reflecting the way in which he was seen as a pitiable and defeated figure rather than a fearsome one. This is particularly true in representations of his frequent appearances of lives of Saints, where he is invariably shown as being defeated and humiliated by the virtue and cunning of the Saint. Generally medieval portrayals show him as bestial and grotesque, hairy, coarse and lacking intelligence. The depictions of demons in Hell and Last Judgments typically show them as a mixture of human and animal or bird, with horns, bird like legs and feet, tails, black skin and red eyes, fangs and long tongues, and with extra faces on various parts of their bodies.

As the way of thinking of the Devil shifted during the Renaissance, so did his portrayal in art. He became less grotesque and even beautiful but more dangerous and intelligent in appearance. In paintings and art from the sixteenth century through to the late nineteenth he has the features and appearance not so much of Pan as Apollo, being shown as a scantily clad and well-formed or handsome figure, beautiful but dark, brooding, and saturnine. He is now often shown as winged and still retaining some of the form and beauty of his previous state as a seraph. This kind of shift is also seen in sculpture. This can be seen clearly if we compare the grotesque and distorted form of the gargoyles of medieval statuary to works such as the *Genie du Mal* (the Genius of Evil) by the nineteenth century Belgian artist Guillaume Geefs. From about the 1880s onwards he comes to be shown as a seductive and charming gentleman, often in evening dress, with pointed eyebrows and saturnine features. In contemporary art however you also see revivals of the figure of the enthroned goat, as many heavy metal albums covers attest.

The other persistent theme in visual representations of the Devil and demons, from the later Middle Ages onwards is that of nightmarish and surreal, fantastic yet horrible portrayals. This can be seen in modern art such as the work of Salvador Dali but in fact begins much earlier in the surreal work of artists such as Hieronymus Bosch (particularly *The Garden of Earthly Delights*) and Pieter Breughel the Elder (such as *The Triumph of Death*). It is particularly common in depictions of the Temptation of St

Anthony or of nightmares, partly because the subject matter is hallucinations or visions. This was a feature of works by a series of artists such as Michelangelo, Hieronymus Bosch, Joos van Craesbeck, Salvador Dali, Max Ernst, and, in perhaps its most arresting and horrific portrayal, Matthias Grunewald. The classic portrayal of the nightmare is that by the eighteenth-century Anglo-Swiss artist Henry Fuseli.

Depictions of the Devil, Hell and the supernatural have remained a prominent feature of art right up to the present day, reflecting the continued fascination of the subject matter. Today it is found most often in the wide genre of fantasy art, which is one of the most vibrant and creative areas of contemporary representational art. In the nineteenth century it was a subject taken by many artists such as William Etty (in *The Destroying Angel and Demons of Evil Interrupting the Orgies of the Vicious and Intemperate*) and John Martin, whose paintings of the citadel of Pandemonium and other scenes from Paradise Lost as well as other paintings of Hell and the Last Judgment led him to be nicknamed 'Hell' Martin (a nickname that had previously been attached to Pieter Breughel the younger). Nineteenth century art such as Martin's made use of Hell and the Devil as ways of examining things such as the impact of industrialism and the challenges both moral and physical that were thrown up by modernity. Historically, over the period from the late Middle Ages onwards, there are a number of artists who are remembered or known primarily for their works depicting Hell and the Devil and demons, such as the two Breughels, Hieronymus Bosch, Matthias Grunewald, Luca Signorelli, Henry Fuseli, and the aforementioned John Martin. The artist who has become particularly linked to this subject matter is the great nineteenth century engraver and illustrator Gustave Dore, because of his illustrations for Dante's *Divine Comedy*.

Artists and writers have always described themes and beliefs and events that are part of the culture they live in. Consequently, given the centrality of the Devil to historical Christian thought and culture, it is no surprise that he has been a prominent subject. Artists are engaged in a two-way process in which they both give form to their society's conception of the principle of personified evil and his actions and also influence and shape the ideas that the people around them and after them have. The way that he has continued to be used and explored by writers and artists in the modern world, when the traditional theology has lost much of its intellectual and cultural hold, shows the continued fascination and capacity of the idea to evoke feelings and move people but also the way that the continued existence of radical evil and of what our ancestors would have bluntly called sin requires exploration and explanation. The Devil still has a part to play in this.

Further Reading

Barker, Clive (2017) *The History of the Devil (The Clive Barker Playscripts)*. Phil and Sarah Stokes.

Bulgakov, Mikhail (2016) *The Master and Margarita*. Penguin.

Christianson, Eric S. and Partridge, Christopher (2008) *The Lure of the Dark Side: Satan and Western Demonology in Popular Culture*. Equinox Books.

Dore, Gustave (1976) *The Dore Illustrations for Dante's "Divine Comedy"*. Dover.

Dore, Gustave (2000) *Dore's Illustrations for "Paradise Lost"*. Dover.

Dostoyevsky, Fyodor & McDuff, David (trans. and ed.) (2003) *The Brothers Karamazov: A Novel in Four Parts and an Epilogue*. Penguin.

Fish, Stanley (1996) "Why We Can't All Just Get Along" *First Things*, February 1st. https://www.firstthings.com/article/1996/02/001-why-we-cant-all-just-get-along

Fowler, Christopher (2003) *Spanky*. Sphere.

Gaiman, Neil (2018) *The Sandman Volume1: Thirtieth Anniversary Edition*. DC Comics.

Gettings, Fred (1988) *Secret Symbolism in Occult Art*. Random House.

Giorgi (2005) *Angels and Demons in Art*. Getty Museum.

Gray, Alasdair (2018) *Hell: Dante's Divine Trilogy Part One*. Canongate Books.

Kastan, David Scott (ed.) (2005) *Marlowe: Doctor Faustus*. Norton Critical Editions.

Kirkpatrick, Robin (trans & ed.) (2006) *Dante: Inferno*. Penguin.

Lehner, Ernst & Johanna (2003) *Devils, Demons, and Witchcraft*. Dover.

Lorenzi, Lorenzo (2006) *Devils in Art: Florence from the Middle Ages to the Renaissance*. Centro Di.

Lorenzi, Lorenzo (2006) *Witches: Exploring the Iconography of the Sorceress and Enchantress*. Centro Di.

Milton, John & Leonard, John (ed). (2003) *Paradise Lost*. Penguin.

Paparoni, Demetrio (2020). *The Art of the Devil: An Illustrated History*. Abrams Books.

Schipper, Bernd U. (2010). "From Milton to Modern Satanism: The History of the Devil and the Dynamics between Religion and Literature". *Journal of Religion in Europe*. **3** 103-124.

Schreck, Nikolas (2000) *The Satanic Screen: An Illustrated Guide to the Devil in Cinema 1896-1999*. Creation Books.

Schreck, Nikolas (ed.) (2001) *Flowers From Hell: A Satanic Reader*. Creation Books.

Tambling, Jeremy (2017) *Histories of the Devil: From Marlowe to Mann and the Manichees*. Palgrave.

Twain, Mark (2019, 1st published 1916) *The Mysterious Stranger*. Penguin.

Updike, John (2007) *The Witches of Eastwick*. Penguin.

Chapter 11. The Devil in Music

Music has been one of the principal art forms for all of human history and in all known societies. It plays a central part in the life of all cultures, including those that follow or descend from the monotheistic faiths, where sacred music has frequently been a part of worship and ritual for centuries. However, in both Christianity and Islam there is a persistent minority tradition that sees music as an impious and corrupting force and associates it with the great tempter, Satan. In Christianity this view is found mainly in radical Protestantism, particularly strict Calvinist churches such as the Free Church of Scotland which until recently did not allow the singing of hymns (as opposed to psalms or paraphrases) or the use of musical instruments during services. Historically hostility to musical performance went along with opposition to acting, dancing, and the theatre generally – that is why one of the first things the Puritans in the Long Parliament did was to close the theatres and ban musical performances. (They also passed the Celebration of Christmas (Abolition) Act). In Islam opposition to all music other than the limited use of the human voice is a prominent feature of contemporary fundamentalist movements such as Salafism but this idea is historically much more prominent than in Christianity and has been debated by the jurists and commentators from a very early date in Islamic history, with major figures taking both sides of the argument. The scholars who argue that music is haram (prohibited) all argue that it is used by the Devil (Iblis) as part of his role in tempting humanity and distracting people from the true path of submission to God, so music in this view is an instrument of the Devil and inspired by him.

The main reason why figures from the two major monotheistic faiths see music as being the work of Satan is its popular association with frivolity, material pleasures, and above all immorality and dissolute behaviour. In particular music (along with dancing) is thought to be conducive to sexual immorality. The actual lifestyles of many musicians both historically and in the contemporary world, and the practices of the artistic subculture of bohemianism and the demimonde have added to this hostility. However, the connection between the Devil and music is not simply a matter of the concerns and prejudices of the devout and is not simply a matter of his using it as an instrument of temptation and seduction. In popular culture and in many actual genres of music the Devil is seen as being closely related to certain kinds and styles of music and musical content. In folklore the Devil is often portrayed as a musician, with his own favourite instrument, the fiddle. A common and recurring folk narrative is that of the fiddler who, either unknowingly or deliberately, enters into a fiddling contest with the Prince of Darkness.

One key point is that the Devil's connection with music in popular culture and much religious thought is not general or indiscriminate but specific and particular. There are certain kinds or genres of music that he favours or inspires, that are in fact his music, while he is indifferent to others or even pained and repulsed by them. One idea is that the Devil cannot abide sacred music (for obvious reasons). In Jewish worship the shofar (a horn, typically made from the horns of a ram) is believed to confuse the Devil and drive him away. So, there are some kinds of music that are actually antithetical to the Devil, and a protection against him.

More generally, popular culture does not associate the Devil with classical or formal music. This last statement does need to be qualified however. The Devil does figure as a subject and character in many pieces of classical music. Thus, he appears frequently in opera, particularly of course in those based on the legend of Faust such as Charles Gounod's *Faust (1859)* and the more recent *Historia von D. Johann Fäusten* by Alfred Schnittke (1995). One classical composer who composed several works in which the Devil figured prominently was Franz Liszt. He produced the *Faust Symphony* (1857) and two works based on Dante's *Divine Comedy*, the *Dante Sonata* (1849) and the *Dante Symphony* (1857), the four *Mephisto Waltzes* (1859–62) and the *Mephisto Polka* (1882-3). Other well-known pieces that allude to the Devil are the *Danse Macabre* of Camille Saint-Saens (1874) and the *Caprice no 13 (The Devil's Chuckle)* (1807) by Niccolo Paganini. A contemporary composer who has produced pieces drawing on classic representations of the Devil is Krzysztof Penderecki who has produced one operatic oratorio based on Milton's *Paradise Lost (Paradise Lost,* 1978), and *The Devils of Loudon* (1978-9) based on the work by Aldous Huxley and the events of the famous witch trial in seventeenth century France.

In addition to works that explicitly deal with Satan or allude to him in their title and content there are some pieces where although he does not appear, he and Hell are key elements of the plot and backdrop. One example is *Don Giovanni,* where the damnation of the Don and the reality of Hell are central parts of the plot. Moreover, there are some composers whose work frequently evokes the occult and dark in its tone and subject matter. One of the best examples is Claude Debussy. Several of his major works, such as *The Sunken Cathedral* explore the themes of damnation and the supernatural and employ a range of sound effects to evoke feelings that combine the beautiful and the eerie. Another classic example is the Russian composer Modest Mussorgsky's tone poem about a witch's sabbat, *A Night on Bald Mountain,* best known from the adaptation by Rimsky-Korsakov that was first performed in 1886. However, while the Devil and related topics are the subject of many formal or classical musical works, these genres are not associated with him in general – they are not seen as being his music. That kind of title is reserved for certain kinds of popular music.

The types of popular music that have come to be associated with the Devil are those already seen as marginal or subversive. This is a matter of three things, the qualities and technical features of the music, its subject matter and lyrical content along with the nature (in modern times) of its stage performance, and in particular its class and ethnic origins and connections. The charge of being 'the devil's music' is levelled at the music produced (at least originally) by the lower classes and marginal or stigmatised social groups, such as Gypsies and, most importantly for recent cultural history, African Americans. Ragtime, jazz, and blues have all been seen as the creation of the Devil, as his music, partly because they have all been accused of inciting immorality and vice (lust in particular but also despair and nihilism and, worst of all, dancing). It was blues above all that came to be known as 'the devil's music' for several generations of anxious and fearful devout Americans.

The folklore or the blues and of famous bluesmen involves the devil in several notorious instances. The best-known story is that of the legendary bluesman and guitarist Robert Johnson, who supposedly gained his extraordinary playing skills by selling his soul to Satan at a crossroads near Dockery Plantation in Louisiana – he was not averse to promoting this story himself. The story had previously been told of other bluesmen, notably Tommy Johnson. Interestingly the great classical violinist Niccolo Paganini was the subject of a very similar story, in which he gained his mastery of the violin through a pact with the Devil. Several of Johnson's best-known songs dealt with the themes of Hell and the supernatural, such as *There's A Hellhound on My Trail*.

As the music of a despised and marginalised social group (black sharecroppers in the Deep South) the respectable were always going to look askance at blues music. The themes and subject matter of the blues also lent itself to this. Drinking and sexual pleasure (and grief) were major topics and the genre was also a form of rebellion or reaction against the status quo of Jim Crow and segregation, rural poverty and hardship. Often it referred to folk magic and its beliefs, as in the well-known Muddy Waters song *Got My Mojo Working* (a mojo is an amulet that protects against hoodoo, the folk magic system of the Mississippi Delta). As such it could easily be seen as subversive and rebellious and linked to the greatest of all rebels, Satan.

Moreover, the music itself has features that give it a quality of sound and emotional effect that leads to that identification. Blues makes extensive use of the F – B tritone interval, which because of its quality and the way it is heard by most people has traditionally been seen as a dissonance (the putting together of sounds that clash and do not naturally fit). As a result, for centuries the tritone has been seen as evoking harshness, unpleasantness, unacceptability, and disorder rather than order and harmony. (This way of thinking about different qualities of sound and connecting them with good and divine purpose on the one hand and evil and rebellion against that purpose on the other is also found explicitly in the work of J. R. R. Tolkien, most notably '*The Music of the Ainur*'). In fact, from as early as the first decade of the eighteenth century and maybe even the medieval period this interval has been nicknamed '*diabolus in musica*' (the devil in music). For many listeners it evokes the eerie or sinister and menacing. It is used in classical music to create precisely that reaction in the listener (the minor key is also typically used, to evoke feelings of loss or sadness). Given that blues made use of this feature and had a harsh and evocative quality in other ways (such as the style of the singing and vocalisation) it is easy to see why some people thought there was something Satanic about the music itself, even disregarding the content. In fact, there was a succession of moral panics in the United States in particular over the evil influence of blues (and also jazz), as corrupting forces that were doing the Devil's work and corrupting the morals of respectable, God-fearing Americans.

This all passed over, along with some of the musical features, into the more mainstream music that grew out of blues – rock and roll (later simply rock music). As is well known rock and roll originally derived from blues and rhythm and blues that were being played increasingly on commercial radio in the 1950s. There were other sources as well, particularly parts of country music (such as Hank Williams) but initially it was seen as very much a case of artists such as Elvis Presley copying and adapting a distinctly African-American genre. Initially it attracted much the same kind of opprobrium that had attached to blues and before then jazz. Gavin Baddeley gives the following representative examples of this reaction "As early as 1956, a Pentecostal preacher in Nottingham, England addressed the rock and roll problem from his pulpit. "The effect of rock and roll is to turn young people into devil worshipers; to stimulate self-expression through sex, to impair nervous stability and destroy the sanctity of marriage". ... In 1956 the *Daily Mail*... declared that rock and roll had "something of the African tom tom and voodoo dance", adding the following day that "it is despicable. It is tribal. And it is from America. It follows rag time, blues, Dixie jazz, hot cha cha and boogie woogie, which surely originated in the jungle. We sometimes wonder whether it is the Negro's revenge" (Baddeley, 1999 p113). (The flag of resistance to rock and roll and indeed all contemporary popular music is still kept flying at the *Daily Mail* by Peter Hitchens)

As rock music developed in the 1960s it became clear that some of the bands involved had a much more explicitly blues-based style than others. It is this particular strand in the wider world of rock and popular music that has come to be associated even more with the Devil and even outright Satanism than blues itself was or is. Interestingly other forms of popular music that share the features of being associated with rebellion, protest, and the culture of African-Americans such as hip-hop and reggae do not nowadays have this connection to the Devil. One of the bands that made use of satanic allusions at an early date was the Rolling Stones, in the song *Sympathy For The Devil* in 1968. In the song, which Mick Jagger says was inspired by Baudelaire, and Bulgakov's *The Master and Margarita*, the Devil recounts the part he has played in a series of events in human history, including the Crucifixion. At the time the Stones met the underground film maker and Crowleyan Kenneth Anger, who introduced them to the occult ideas he had been exploring as part of the California counterculture that had produced the Church of Satan, although this was more of a passing phase than a longer-term influence on the band. The general point though was that as the 1960s progressed popular music and the counterculture began to take a darker turn, at least as far as the presentation of style and music was concerned. Subsequently other rock bands such as Led Zeppelin became associated with the occult by fans and the media (in their case because of the well-known interest in Crowley and Thelema of their lead guitarist, Jimmy Page).

Initially though, the adoption of themes and content that referred to things such as witchcraft and the Devil happened mainly with bands from what we may call the hippy counterculture side of popular music. One example was Coven who in 1969 produced an entire album on the theme of witchcraft and Devil worship with the title *Witchcraft Destroys Minds and Reaps Souls*. However, during the 1970s occult and overtly Satanic imagery, references and subject matter, and stylistic features came to be strongly associated with hard rock. A number of prominent bands made extensive use of symbolism and imagery as well as lyrics and titles, that alluded to the Devil and the occult and pushed further down the route begun by people such as the Rolling Stones and Led Zeppelin. Two of the best known were Blue Oyster Cult and the Australian hard rock band AC/DC. BOC used a hermetic symbol on all of their album covers and had several songs with suggestive content, particularly on the album *Agents of Fortune*. AC/DC had numbers such as *Highway to Hell* and *Hells Bells*. A British band who became pioneers in this respect were Black Widow, with their frontman Jim Gannon, most notably in the 1970 album *Sacrifice*.

It was though the British hard rock band Black Sabbath who effectively created a distinctive genre out of the more general category of hard rock, and linked that genre closely to ideas and images of the supernatural and above all the Devilish and Satanic. The genre is of course heavy metal. The connection and association of heavy metal music with the Devil and the supernatural is now so close and well known that if anyone sees an album or compact disc cover or promotional poster or tee shirt with imagery of the Devil, Satanism or the occult they will be very confident that they already know what kinds of music and sounds it is promoting. It will not be country, or dance, or folk music or even mainstream rock, much less pop or hip hop. It will be heavy metal, with a distinctive sound and often vocals. One feature of the sound is the regular use of the above mentioned tritone or *diabolus in musica* – something pioneered (or in this case revived) like so much else by

Black Sabbath. (There is also regular use of power chords – perfect fourths and fifths for the technically minded).

Black Sabbath's lead guitarist (and the key figure in the band) Tony Iommi was the one who introduced the use of the distinctive interval. The supernatural subject matter of many of the band's songs came more from their bass player and main lyricist Geezer Butler. From their first eponymous album onwards, there was always at least one song with a supernatural or demonic theme while later there was an entire album organised around it (*Headless Cross* in 1989). Their stage show, like that of Blue Oyster Cult, made use of symbols such as inverted crosses, and pyrotechnics to evoke the image of Hell. So successful were they that other bands rapidly adopted their style or formed with the aim of developing it and an entire genre and subculture emerged. In this genre, as said, the Devil and images associated with him, became a central aspect of the performance and subject matter of the groups, with examples such as Demon with tracks such as *Night of the Demon* from 1981 and *Don't Break the Circle*, and *Beyond the Gates of Hell* from 1982. Bands such as KISS carried on the tradition but that tended to develop into a deliberately camp and over the top kind of sensibility, epitomized by later groups such as Motley Crue. The more straightforward line of descent came through what became known as New Wave of British Heavy Metal (NWOBHM) with bands such as Judas Priest, Saxon, Tygers of Pan Tang, Iron Maiden, Girlschool, Angelwitch, and Raven. Several of these bands such as Iron Maiden put on elaborate themed stage shows with spectacular imagery, often of an infernal type, not to mention numbers such as the classic *Number of the Beast*. There was then a new source of inspiration for heavy metal in the shape of punk and this led to thrash or speed metal, typified by bands such as Metallica and Slayer, who again used much of the imagery and subject matter introduced by Black Sabbath and subsequently developed by the later bands.

However, for all of these bands the references to the Devil in titles and lyrics, and the stage shows and cover art with their allusions to the supernatural were essentially a marketing ploy. By annoying the respectable, and horrifying parents, they gained the bands publicity and increased sales of recordings and concert tickets. However, there was no question of the musicians actually believing in this and they were often bemused by the way many observers and, crucially, their fans did take it seriously. What happened though was the emergence of a subgenre from within thrash metal where these themes not only became more prominent but also were increasingly taken seriously rather than being simply a marketing ploy. The key event was the album *Black Metal* by the British band Venom, issued in 1982 (their debut the previous year had been entitled *Welcome to Hell*). The emergent sub-genre of black metal has become the one that has the most truly hard core and often sincere explorers of Satan in music. One British exponent was Cradle of Filth, who produced in 1993 what must be the most offensive marketing tee shirt of all time (with the slogan Jesus Is A C**t). Although black metal first appears in Britain and has representatives there and in the United States the style and genre are most associated with Scandinavia, with most of the leading bands coming from the various Scandinavian countries, notably Sweden and Finland.

One of the earliest was the Danish band Mercyful Fate, formed in 1981. Their lead singer, King Diamond, was and is a card-carrying LaVeyan Satanist and their second album *Don't Break the Oath* was a thematic one about the summoning and evocation of evil powers. After this the band dissolved but King Diamond went on to form an eponymous band and have an enormous influence on the emerging genre. (Among other things he introduced the widespread practice of wearing 'corpse face paint' on stage). Subsequent groups in the tradition that formed in that decade included Celtic Frost from Switzerland, Kreator from Germany, Ghost and Bathory from Sweden, and Morbid Angel and Deicide in the United States. Deicide's frontman, Glen Benton, is an outspoken critic of Christianity from a Left-Hand Path perspective and has branded an inverted cross into his forehead – there really is no going back from that! In the 1990s there was a huge growth in the scene in Scandinavia and elsewhere. Among some of the contemporary bands that feature overt Satanic content and themes are Behereit, Archgoat, and Behexen (Finland), Dark Funeral, Watain, DIssection (Sweden), and Gorgoroth (Norway). Outside Scandinavia there are bands such as Destroyer 666 (Australia), Belphegor (Austria), Behemoth (Poland), and Goatwhore (US). Study of the output of bands like these reveals an abundance of Satanic themes and symbols, such as demons, scenes from Hell, goats heads, and the well known Baphomet image (as well as much imagery from Tolkien and Norse paganism).

Norway though was what we may call the epicentre of early black metal. The central figure was the lead guitarist of the band

Mayhem, Oystein Aarseth, usually referred to by his stage name Euronymous. His posthumous album of 1994, *De Mysteriis Dom Sathanas* is widely regarded as the most influential black metal album ever. (The title is an incorrect Latin translation of the phrase "Of the Mysteries of the Lord Satan") Helvete, the shop and centre he ran in Oslo after setting it up in 1991, became a meeting place for musicians and groups interested not only in the style of music but also in vehement opposition to all of the conventional pieties of social democratic Scandinavia, such as socialism, democracy, the welfare state, and Christianity. Many were interested in Old Norse paganism and neopagan revivals but both atheist and theistic Satanism were also common, partly as a way of rejecting convention in as dramatic a way as possible. Among the bands that formed what became known as the 'black metal scene' in Norway were Carpathian Forest, Darkthrone, Emperor, Satyricon, Immortal, Thorns, and Burzum, the last a one-person project of Varg Vikernes.

Between 1992 and 1995 members of the scene including Vikernes were involved in a campaign of arson attacks on Norwegian 'stave' churches (so called because of their form of construction from wood) with anything up to fifty-six attacks. On 10th August 1993 Vikernes and Snorre 'Blackthorn' Ruch (of Thorns) murdered Euronymous at his apartment in Oslo. They were arrested a week later and eventually were sentenced. Vikernes received a sentence of twenty-one years (the maximum allowed in Norway) for the murder as well as for three instances of arson attacks on churches and the possession of 100 pounds of explosives. Blackthorn received eight years as an accessory for murder. This brought the scene to an abrupt halt and some of the people involved began to emphasise neopaganism rather than Satanism. However, most of them continued their musical careers and have been highly productive, and as mentioned earlier there are still many bands, including some of those from the early 1990s, that are active and still producing music and artwork with distinctly Satanic content.

One of those who continued to have an active career was Vikernes, who recorded two albums while in prison (he was released in 2009). He was one of those who came to emphasise neopaganism rather than Satanism, although his ideological hostility to contemporary society and social democracy remains as strong as ever. He now lives in France and until recently had a popular YouTube channel called *Thulean Perspectives*. His two prison albums and subsequent releases show a shift from heavy metal to dark ambient music. That genre has also got strong associations with the supernatural and themes of horror but it lacks the explicit employment of images of the Devil and use of topics associated with him that are found in heavy metal and particularly black metal.

The other genre which has sometimes had supernatural connections or links to ritual magic is industrial music, particularly in the works of Genesis Breyer P-Orridge, who virtually created the genre through his band Throbbing Gristle. P-Orridge went on in 1981 to found an occult group called Thee Temple ov Psychic Youth (TOPY) but this was focused mainly on chaos magic of the kind described briefly in Chapter five. P-Orridge had met Anton LaVey but although interested in his ideas, their main influence was the early twentieth century British occultist Austin Osman Spare. The industrial band that has the most explicitly Satanic content to its work and publicity is The Electric Hellfire Club, whose leading figure Thomas Thorn is another card-carrying LaVeyan Satanist. Industrial music has fed into a number of emerging musical genres that display an interest in magic, occultism and paganism, in particular neofolk and martial industrial music. The Devil however does not feature, although more general occultism and neopaganism do.

Not surprisingly, the turn taken by heavy metal bands in the 1980s and subsequently had the people who had always thought there was something Devil-inspired about the music feeling that their worst fears had been realised. There was a serious and organised backlash in the United States in particular, led by the redoubtable Tipper Gore (wife of the then US Senator Al Gore). In 1985 along with Susan Baker (whose husband James Baker was then the US Treasury Secretary) she founded the Parents Music Resource Center to campaign for labels on music with profane or sexual and Satanic content. At the same time a whole series of urban myths about heavy metal and hard rock music began to circulate, such as that playing Led Zeppelin's *Stairway to Heaven* backwards revealed Satanic lyrics or that Judas Priest's version of the Spooky Tooth song *Better By You, Better Than Me* contained subliminal messages that prompted young people to commit suicide. The last myth actually led to Judas Priest facing a civil trial in Nevada in 1990 – the case was eventually dismissed. More seriously there was also the massive Satanic Abuse panic described in chapter six. Among other things this led to a Channel 4 documentary making very serious allegations of child abuse against Genesis P-Orridge, which turned out to be totally baseless and involve material that Channel 4 themselves had sponsored, but which led them to relocate to the US. The reaction against heavy metal (and other genres of popular music such as rap and hip hop) led by Tipper Gore did not have such grave results, although it was an irritation for some bands. For the genre as a whole it probably acted as an encouragement to been even more outrageous, and stimulated purchases by disaffected young people rather than checking them.

Although the level of interest in and overt commitment to Satan and his works has declined even within black metal, there is still widespread use of Satanic imagery within heavy metal in general and, as the list of bands given earlier indicates, a continuing body of bands and musicians who identify more strongly with the figure of Satan, whether as an actual entity or (more often) a symbol of rebellion and rejection of the conventional morality. In addition to the bands already named we could mention ones such as Acheron, Nunslaughter, Marduk, Nifelheim, and Horna. Simply browsing through streaming sites such as Spotify will reveal a wealth of Satanic goats, Baphomet heads, inverted crucifixes, and portrayals of demons and Hell. Music is very powerful because of its ability to generate powerful sentiments and feelings and to move the listener in dramatic and unexpected ways. It all the more powerful for being direct and unmediated, unlike words (whether spoken or printed) or even visual images. As such it has a long standing relation with both authority on the one hand and rebellion and protest on the other. Those who fear the Devil and his always present but often not seen influence have frequently thought that music is one of his chosen instruments. The inverse of this in the modern world has been for people such as artists and particularly musicians who wish to shock and provoke for commercial reasons or to dramatise a more serious alienation from the respectable status quo to adopt Satan as the great symbol or rebellion and denial of conventional morality. The role of the Devil in parts of contemporary popular music, whether as a marketing ploy or as something more sincere, is perhaps the most dramatic instance of the way he is still the great figure of denial and rejection, disturbing yet fascinating, and for some inspiring.

Further reading
Baddeley, Gavin (1999). *Lucifer Rising: Sin, Devil Worship, and Rock and Roll*. Plexus.

Baddeley, Gavin (2002) *Goth Chic: A Connoisseur's Guide to Dark Culture.* Plexus Publishing.

Baddeley, Gavin & Filth, Dani (2010). *The Gospel of Filth: A Bible of Decadence and Darkness.* Fab Press.

Corupe, Paul (2016) *Satanic Panic: Pop-Cultural Paranoia in the 1980s.* Fab Press.

Klein, S. L. (2014) *The Devil's Music: From Lydian Modes to Heavy Metal.* Create Space.

Moynihan, Michael & Sonderlind, Didrik (2003, 1st published 1998) *Lords of Chaos: The Bloody Rise of the Satanic Metal Underground.* Feral House.

Patterson, Dyal (2014) *Black Metal: Evolution of the Cult.* Feral House.

Purcell, Natalie J. (2003) *Death Metal Music: The Passion and Politics of a Subculture.* McFarland.

Taylor, Troy (2019) *A Song of Dance and Death: Magic, Murder, Mayhem, and the Diabolical Notes of the Devil's Music.* Whitechapel Productions.

Walser, Robert (2014) *Running With the Devil: Power, Gender, and Madness in Heavy Metal Music.* Wesleyan University Press.

Weinstein, Deena (2000) *Heavy Metal: The Music and Its Culture.* Da Capo.

Weinstein, Deena (1998) *Heavy Metal: A Cultural Sociology.* New Lexington Press.

The best way to explore this topic is to listen to the actual music, which, thanks to streaming, is much easier.

Conclusion

The Devil does not loom as large in the minds and culture of today as he did three or four hundred years ago but he is still an immediately recognisable figure and he appears frequently in the popular culture of our times. Belief in his real existence and activity is strongly adhered to by a persistent minority and ideas connected with him, such as that of a conspiracy directed by him against all that is good retain their fascination and can still have dramatic real-world effects on both law enforcement and politics. He is also still taken seriously as a concept and even as an entity by a surprisingly large number of scholars, theologians and philosophers, even if a lot of the theology has been stripped away. Simultaneously he and many of the creatures once associated with him, from witches to vampires and werewolves, have been re-evaluated so that for many he and they are at least anti-heroes, maybe even actual heroes. The onetime symbol of ultimate evil has thus become for some a positive figure. Despite that though, belief in the existence of radical evil remains pervasive, given the evidence for its existence, and personification of that phenomenon as a way of explaining it is attractive to many, maybe increasingly so.

Historically the Devil cannot be separated from the monotheistic religions. He appears as a defined figure in the monotheistic religions of the Middle East as does the fundamental concept that he embodies, that of a malign and malevolent adversary, a spiritual power of darkness and destruction. As a defined figure with a biography and part to play in history he arose or emerged in Christianity, as the new faith made use of and amended its inheritance from Judaism. The idea later appears in a similar but not identical form in the third monotheistic faith, that of Islam although it never attained the central importance there that it did in Christianity. This meant a major change in the way people thought about and understood both human nature and the nature of the natural world and humanity's place in it. This can be seen by comparing the commonalities in those respects between Judaism, Christianity, and Islam, and the approaches found in the surviving non monotheistic civilisations in East and South Asia. As the monotheistic civilisations developed, and went on to supplant and overcome several of the major pagan religions of the ancient world during the Middle Ages and later, so the Devil became a central part of their culture and world view. Changes in those civilisations led to their understanding of the Devil altering, as we have seen.

There are signs that in Europe and North America at least we are seeing the gradual demise of the monotheistic Western civilisation. One of the signs of this is changes in the part that the Devil plays in intellectual and cultural life and the way he is understood both by the educated and the general public. This does raise a major question. If, as Nietzsche argued, God is dead (meaning that people no longer believe in him and, more importantly, that the idea of God is no longer the way people make sense of the world and events) then can the Devil survive? One view is that it was belief in the Devil and his servants and allies that faded first and that this prefigured the decline of faith in God and the faith that Matthew Arnold identified in "*Dover Beach*". If that is true then he is now a survival of a mental world that is slowly losing its hold on the Western mind and as such he is moving steadily from the category of the serious and important to that of the entertaining and ironic. If that is the case then he will suffer the fate of pagan deities, to exist as a character in fictions and tales because of his power as an archetype but not in a way that is taken seriously or that will actually influence the decisions and choices people make.

A related argument is that we are seeing the first intimations of a revival of the ways of thinking that monotheism supplanted during the periods of late Antiquity and the Middle Ages. In this way of thinking the so-far peripheral but vital revivals of paganism, and the appearance of invented pagan traditions such as Wicca is a foretaste of their eventual revival. In that case the Devil will cease to be understood as he has been for two thousand years because that way of thinking only makes sense in the framework of the monotheistic and particularly the Christian view and account of the world. He may still survive but will be reconfigured to become one of the dark or destructive gods that were a feature of traditional paganism, not venerated but also not malevolent. Things such as the clear reassessment of the Devil and his actions and of the values associated with him that we have seen since the later nineteenth century can be made to fit into this story, as signs of the weakening hold of the Christian monotheistic vision on our minds.

The other side of this is the argument that, even if explicit Christian monotheism has lost its hold on the educated and popular mind in Europe and North America, it has not done so elsewhere in the world, where traditional Christianity, and Islam go from strength to strength. Moreover, a persuasive argument is that our modes and structures of thinking are still shaped by the Christian thinking that appeared in the ancient world and were worked out by a succession of thinkers from around Augustine onwards. For people such as Tom Holland we still think and understand the world in Christian categories, even if the actual beliefs have perished and the ideas are given a secular lick of paint (so that the apocalypse becomes the proletarian revolution or the Singularity for example) (Holland, 2019). If that is true then the Devil will survive, even if not in the form he had when Christian belief was overt and conscious. The basic idea will persist but be understood in secular form (with actual human beings or institutions taking on the role of the Devil as the malevolent source of evil). This will actually be a less useful and effective belief and in many ways more harmful but it would still exist, because it helps to make sense of things that otherwise are incomprehensible.

This explains the continued use of the metaphors of Hell and the Devil, or even the use of them as actual entities, to make sense of the phenomena of radical evil, spite and malice both at an individual and a mass level. Strangely, the adversary may have a better chance of surviving and thriving in modern secularism than the idea of a providential source of good, although people say in polls that they are more likely to believe in the latter than the former (perhaps because the idea of a world with an active power for bad but not for good is too disturbing). This idea and the previous one that we are living in the twilight of a two-thousand year old civilisation, are not incompatible or exclusive. They can be combined by the argument that the process will take a long time (as the demise of Antiquity did, several hundred years in fact). In that case the Devil may survive for several hundred years more, even if he fades away or is transformed during that time.

The obvious alternative is that the Devil will experience a sudden revival and that people will once again start to take him seriously and to fear his power and machinations in the way they once did. We should not reject that possibility. Obviously believers cannot while remaining true to their faith accept that God no longer exists or has agency, even if nobody believes in him or worships Him. Similarly, they will continue to believe in the Devil, even if he has successfully persuaded most that he is imaginary. Christianity as a faith has been written off before over the last two hundred years and it would be a brave man or woman who would bet against its reviving and its teachings once again being widely believed. In that case we can confidently expect the Adversary to also make a comeback and the Prince of Darkness to once again be thought of as a power and presence both real and fearsome. In any event, much of the history of the last two thousand years or more cannot be understood without knowing about the Devil and understanding how people thought about him while the present world contains many examples of both his continued fascination and, for those who believe, his continued actions in the latest stage of a cosmic combat.

Further Reading
Holland, Tom (2019) *Dominion: The Making of the Western Mind.* Little, Brown.

Index

Art, representation of the Devil in, 54, 151–155, surreal and fantastical 154.
Augustine, St 31–2, 48, 114.

Brothers Karamazov 147–149.

Crowley, Aleister 69, 130–132.

Dante Alighieri and *Divine Comedy* 84–86, 143–144.
Dark Gods and deities, 1, 17–18, 19. Yahweh as one 18.
Demons and the demonic, 3, 35, 78, and Chapter 7 *passim*
    original conception of 91–94,
    hierarchy of 95,
    in Islam 95–96,
    in Judaism 96–97,
    and demonology 97–98, 102,
    and ritual magic 98–100,
    physical manifestation 100–101,
    incubi and succubi 101,
    possession 101–102.
Demonic conspiracy 3, 13, 48, 112–114, 128–129, 166–167.
The Devil
    not found in all religions 1,
    and malevolence, 1, 8–9,
    and theodicy 9–11.
    as adversary, 1, 11, 23–24,
    as rebel 11, 23–26, 65, 94–95, 147,
    as Dark Lord 49.
    not always going to exist 1,
    not always evil 11
    origins and creation of the idea, Chapter 2 *passim*, 2, 20–21, 23, 26
    changes in content of the idea, 3
    a person or entity 7–8
    His knowledge 12–13, 49–50, 66,
    as tempter and seducer 13, 20, 33, 37–38, 48–49,
    epiphets and associations 12–13, 36,
    in Islam 28–9,
    and theories of salvation 31–32.
    physical appearance 34–36, 49, 152–153

Evil,
    and the Devil 5, 6, 70–71.
    nature and types of 5–6, radical evil 6.
    and malevolence 7–8, 9.
    and theodicy 10–11.
    and corruption of the human will 12,
    and the axial age 18–19
    in Zoroastrianism 19.
    increased awareness off during the Renaissance 47–48,

Fairies 95, as minor demons 103
Faust, 50–51.
Film,
    the Devil in 150,
    Vampires in 105,
    Werewolves in 106.

Golden Dawn, Hermetic order of the 130.
Grimoires 99.

Hell, Chapter 6 *passim*
   combines two different notions of the afterlife, 75-77, 81.
   formation of the idea 78-80.
   and the Devil 13, 26, 80,
   as a physical location 81-82
   as a state of mind 86-87.
   as a way of capturing features of modernity 87-88.
   in Islam 82, 84-85.
   in vision narratives 83-84.
   in Dante's Divine Comedy 84-86.
Harrowing of Hell 32
Hellfire Clubs 68.
Hermeticism 40-41, 51-52, 64.

Kabbalah, 64,

Last Judgment 26, 33, 152.
LaVey, Anton 133-135.
Levi, Eliphas 129.
Libertinism 66-68.
Lilith 96-97.
Limbo and Purgatory 80-81,
Literature, the Devil in, Chapter 10, *passim*,
   in Dante 143-144,
   in Marlowe 144,
   in Milton 145-147,
   in *Brothers Karamazov* 147-149,
   in *The Master and Margerita* 149-150,
   in other works of fiction 150.
   Portrayals of Hell in 83-86.

Marlowe, Christopher 51, 84-87, 144.
Medieval Era, the Devil in, Chapter 3 *passim*
   consolidation of the idea and theology 31-32, 34-36, 37-38.
   physicality of the Devil and Hell at this time 32, 35-36.
   portrayed and understood as defeated 36-37.
   new narratives appear 34-35
   role in popular culture of 34, 38
   ritual magic in 38-41
   portrayal in art of period 151-152.
Modernity, the Devil in, Chapter 5 *passim*,
   decline in literal belief in modern times, 3, 57-59,
   persistence in belief in the Devil in modernity 60-62,
   transformation into positive figure 64-6,
   and Hell 87-88.
Morning of the Magicians 132.
Music, connection with the Devil Chapter 11 passim,
   religious hostility to music as the Devil's work 157-158,
   and F-B tritone 160,
   in classical music 158,
   in blues and African American music 159-161,
   in rock and roll 161-162,
   in heavy metal 162-166,
   in black metal 164-166,
   in industrial music 166

Occultism, 69-70, 128-130, left and right-hand paths 131. See also Hermeticism.

Pagels, Elaine 28.
Paradise Lost, 64-65, 145-147.
Parsons, Jack 131-132.

Renaissance, the Devil in, Chapter 4 *passim*
    context of the period 45–47
    increased consciousness of evil during the 47–48
    change in the idea of the Devil during 48–51
    and Hell, 84–87
    and ritual magic 51–54
    portrayal in art 153.
    understood as a Renaissance Prince 49
Ritual magic, 38–40, 51–54, 62–63, 68, 98–100, 136.
Russell, Jeffrey Burton 27–28.

Satanic Abuse panic 119–122, and popular music 166–167.
Modern Satanism, Laveyan (Church of Satan) 133–137, theistic (Temple of Set et al) 136–138, extent 138–139.
Shakespeare, William, portrayal of malevolent characters 7.

Temptation of St Anthony 33.

Vampire 103–105.
Vikernes, Varg 164–166.

Watchers, the 21–23, 66.
Werewolves 105–106.
Witches and witchcraft chapter 8 *passim*,
    universal belief in 109–110,
    Medieval Church's attitude towards 110–111,
    change in belief 111–114,
    and witch-hunt 114–116,
    and the Devil 116–118,
    decline in elite belief in 118–119,
    persistence of transformed popular belief 119–120,
    appearance and revaluation as Wicca 122–124.

Zoroastrianism,
    as the origin of the idea of a malevolent power, 19.
    impact on Judaism 20
    idea of Hell in 78.